M000195407

DO A DAY

How to Live a Better Life
Every Day

*How I overcame challenges, lost 100 pounds, ran a marathon,
changed my diet and learned to help others live a better life,
every day*

BRYAN FALCHUK

newbodi.espublishing
Boston, Massachusetts, USA

Copyright © 2017 Bryan Falchuk
All rights reserved.
ISBN: 0-9985492-0-7
ISBN-13: 978-0-9985492-0-0

For My Son, My Motivation

The information and ideas presented in this book are not intended as medical advice or as a substitute for medical counseling. Always consult your physician before beginning any exercise and nutrition program. If you choose not to obtain the consent of your physician and/or work with your physician throughout the duration of your time using the recommendations in this book, you are agreeing to accept full responsibility for your actions and recognize that despite all precautions on the part of the author and/or publisher there are risks of injury or illness which can occur in connection with, or as a result of, use or misuse of the exercises, advice, diets and/or information found in this book. You expressly assume such risks and waive, relinquish and release any claim, which you may have against the author or publisher.

CONTENTS

"The revolution started with a revelation."

—Bryan Falchuk
(that's me)

I. THE DO A DAY PHILOSOPHY

Life is full of hardships, difficult moments and amazing experiences. Some of these challenges can be overwhelming, so we don't do them as well as we wish we could, or don't do them at all. We want better for ourselves. We miss out. We are unhappy, sick or worse.

But what if there were a way to get through anything you might face? What if you could more than just "get through" it, but actually *achieve and grow*?

There is, and I call it **Do a Day**.

It's a simple premise that is incredibly powerful and empowering. It's at the heart of how I transformed my life and have achieved several "impossible" goals along the way, like the Day I ran a marathon. It's how I know that nothing I've worked for is fleeting, nor is the effort of anything I pursue too much for me to handle.

In June 2011, I was at an all-time low in my life. My wife had become extremely sick and no one knew what was wrong. Doctors had carried out scores of tests and tried a handful of treatments, but with each new hope came more disappointment as the treatments missed the mark and my wife's rapid downward spiral continued. I was struggling to cope. I'd grown fat again, reaching 222 pounds, or about 40 to 50 pounds over a healthy weight for my frame. I was run-down, and I had become depressed. To make it worse, my young son, barely two and a half, had a front-row seat to his parents' collapse.

I'd tried to get myself out of the rut. I knew my wife needed me to be strong and keep myself together, but no matter what I tried I just slipped back into a negative loop. Every pep talk I gave myself was quickly undone by the gravity of my situation. Every time I had a sense of duty to care for my wife and be there for my son, I'd be crushed by the idea that I'd lose her and be on my own to parent a child, who'd have to live with the impact of losing his mother at such a young age. My old approaches that focused on willpower and obligation were no match for the gravity of everything.

However, unlike any other attempt I had made at transformation, the one that I started on July 1st that year stuck. And unlike any prior attempts, it was not hard work. It wasn't overbearing or scary. It was empowering: each successive step built from the last in a virtuous cycle rather than a vicious one.

This transformation's enduring success cannot be attributed to luck, grit, magic or coincidence. There are specific reasons I was able to overcome barriers, break patterns and achieve what I wanted for myself and my family. I lost 50 pounds, and became a true athlete who completed several major endurance events like century rides[1] and a marathon. I also stood by my wife through her long struggle to save herself and have been there for my son, who is an amazing and inspiring young boy. My transformation has not been fleeting; I remain a changed person more than five years later, and have continued to grow, evolve and thrive.

Now you know a little about my own struggles, but there is so much more to it. I shared my story because I want you to realize that I — like most people — have faced great challenges. However, I've found a way to overcome many of the things you may also face in your life. Though our situations may differ in many ways, there is a common thread of understanding that resonates when we find ourselves at dark points in our lives. Through the path I've blazed for myself, I learned a way to breakthrough and advance that translates broadly.

---

[1] 100 mile bike rides, the first of which I finished in the lead group despite next to no training or even experience on a road bike.

How do I know it translates? I'm not just guessing — I've seen it myself. As a Certified Personal Trainer and Behavioral Change Specialist I've coached and mentored many people using the Do a Day approach that I share in this book. I've seen it work in many different situations and across all types of people, and have learned an effective way to share it so it inspires your own success.

Personally, throughout my professional career, I've worked in Corporate America, becoming a C-level executive at an insurance company, managing large teams, big budgets and challenging competitive conditions. I've used Do a Day with my own staff and others I work with to help them succeed in their careers and contribute to the overall success of the organization. So while I've used it myself, I've also been fortunate to have many opportunities to help others with Do a Day in varied areas of their lives.

I've structured this book into three sections to help you easily and effectively apply Do a Day to your life. In the first section (*The Do a Day Philosophy*), I share the specific and clear philosophy that has brought me lasting success. The second section (*The "Why" & "What" to Do: Motivation & Goals*) helps you develop the foundation you need to not only know what to do but why you're doing it in the first place. And lastly, the third section (*Take Action: How to Do a Day*) gives you specific examples of how to put the Do a Day approach in place in to your life to achieve your goals such as having a better Diet,[2] reaching a higher level of physical fitness and living an all-around better life.

It all starts with a Day — one single Day. All you need is to decide to **Do a Day.**

---

[2] Why did I capitalize Diet? Find out more in *Do a Day to Eat Well*.

DAY 1.
THE FIRST STEP

In this chapter, I will introduce Do a Day to you so you can understand what it is, and learn about where it came from. That will set you up to start seeing how it can work in a variety of situations and challenges I've faced over the years that helped grow Do a Day into something that can help anyone.

Do a Day is a philosophy you can apply for success in any area of your life: health and wellness, family, work, happiness and more; really, the only limitations are ones you impose.

Do a Day is not a life hack, shortcut or fast fix. It is a mindset. It is an approach to living your life that inevitably permeates every aspect of living it. It is a system that works; I am the living proof. Behind this movement is a boy who grew up obese, depressed and anxious. That formed a man who could be very overwhelmed by the sheer weight of things despite weight no longer being an issue for him. And of course, "he" is me.

When I was obese, I consistently found myself overwhelmed by the notion of just how much weight I had to lose, how long it would take, how much effort, both physical and mental, would be required and how much I'd have to give up. I had nearly 100 pounds to drop, which could be a non-starter for most people.

That idea absolutely floored me and pushed me back into my dark corner, where the depression I lived with could only be comforted by food. This was a vicious cycle, which only meant the number of pounds to lose increased, making the size of the task that much bigger. To compound matters, in addition to turning to food for comfort, I also really despised the things that were needed to lose weight: diet and exercise. I felt restricted by the rules of various diets, which took away my enjoyment of food. I was tired from the effort that was so far beyond what I perceived my abilities to be. I felt embarrassed by how bad I was at sports and exercise compared to everyone around me.

The notion of shedding all the weight I needed to lose seemed impossible to me. It just couldn't be done; that sense of impossibility only made me feel worse. Add to that the pressure and judgment I felt from family, friends and even strangers. I imagined enduring even more humiliation when I failed yet again to lose weight and in fact just got bigger. This had been my pattern so far. Why would it ever be different?

It would be different because this time I saw it differently.

While the number of pounds I had to lose was overwhelming and the fear of failing was paralyzing, the reality was that I didn't have to lose all the weight at once. **I just had to lose a pound at a time**. Once I realized this, I felt this massive burden disappear. I suddenly felt like I actually could succeed. And I didn't have to do it for my parents who were unhappy and worried about my physical condition; for my siblings who tormented me over my weight; for bullies at school, in my neighborhood or at summer camp; or for anyone else. The only person I had to do it for was *me*.

One pound at a time, for me.

That's when the idea of Do a Day was born. You can do anything for a day. A day doesn't have the crushing weight of a lifetime, the long road of hundreds of miles or the daunting goal of losing 100 pounds.

Do a Day is about being mindful of the current task in front of you — that one little thing at that one little moment and nothing else. It's about not worrying over the next thing you have to do or how it fits into your life. Just look at right now, today, and do it. The sum of Doing these Days becomes your new life.

The Do a Day concept isn't as passive or broad as "live your life one day at a time." That expression is about getting by, gritting through it or enduring something tough. Instead, Do a Day is *purposeful* and *proactive*. It's how you achieve, overcome, conquer and change. And ultimately: *succeed.*

You've likely heard the quote from Chinese philosopher Lao Tzu, who said, "A journey of a thousand miles starts with a single step." Do a Day is about taking that first step. Just that one step. Then, tomorrow, you take the next step without focusing on the overwhelming enormity of the remaining steps. We walk each one in turn. Over the days, weeks, months and years, each step joins with the ones before it to become a mile, ten miles, 100 miles and finally 1,000 miles, until your journey is complete and you are better for having made it.

So, let's start today and Do a Day with this book. Each chapter introduces one idea at a time. Turn the page and start reading: one page, then another, then another ...

It doesn't matter if you feel like you won't have the time to finish the book, if you think it will take you weeks or if you doubt whether the ideas will work for you. Just accept the idea of doing something right now, today.

Now, turn the page, and let's go Do a Day together.

THE END OF THE DAY

Let's recap the key ideas from *Day 1. The First Step*:

- Do a Day is an approach to achieving, overcoming and succeeding in the face of challenges that seem too big to tackle

- Do a Day is about focusing on what you have to do right here, right now to succeed without the burden of past mistakes or the gravity of all that lies ahead

- Do a Day is proactive and purposeful, where your actions and choices add up to your success

DAY 2.
BEFORE MY DAWN

In this chapter, I want to share my childhood with you so you can see what factors came together to define the man I would become. There may be things you directly identify with and other things you won't, but you should understand some of the factors that shaped my values, feelings and situation. Beyond my specific situation, you should also think about what you experienced during your formative years, and how these events shaped who you are and the challenges you face today that you can use Do a Day to overcome.

My childhood was one many Americans can probably relate to. I'm the youngest of four kids with parents who got divorced when I was pretty young. Like an increasing number of kids these days, I was overweight starting around age four or five. I then became truly obese as I finished elementary school, peaking somewhere north of 250 pounds in high school (I stopped weighing myself after hitting 248, because I couldn't face the numbers anymore).

There were a lot of things in my childhood that didn't make me feel good. It was a slow burn more than any specific, shocking trauma. There were some tough, confusing times as my parents' marriage came apart in my first few years. With my father working a ton and generally seeming stressed and impatient on a daily basis, and my mother blowing hot and cold from one moment to the next, I didn't really feel parental love and comfort with the sort of consistency and dependability little kids really need. They had big things on their plate, so I certainly don't blame them for any of it. They did the best they could with *their* situation, but the impact of *my* situation was the same regardless of my understanding or not blaming. I needed the kind of love and comfort really little kids just need and yearn for. To put it plainly, in my formative years when I needed support, comfort, guidance and stability, my needs weren't satisfied by my family life.

I sought that comfort and solace in food. I think a lot of kids turn to food when they aren't getting sufficient comfort and support at home. Young children aren't emotionally mature enough or self-reliant enough to solve for this need in ways that an adult might. Food, especially the processed and unhealthy variety, is accessible to most children, tastes good, doesn't judge you and never turns you away. Food was comforting; it made me feel good, brought zero judgment, took no effort to have and was always there for me.

Our cupboards were stocked with cookies and other goodies, and there was always soda in our fridge. With four kids, my parents didn't really monitor what each of us was eating. As my weight increased, my parents started paying attention and trying to control my eating, but it was too late. I had developed enough food-sneaking skills to get around their efforts to protect me from myself. Worse than the sneaking skills, I had subconsciously developed dependence.

Eating wasn't just about physical fuel to me, but emotional fuel. Actually, it was probably only about the emotional fuel since I never really let myself get physically hungry. I ate primarily to feel better. Eating would satiate my anxiety and need for comfort for a few hours (at most), but then I needed more food to continue to feel better. Despite feeling better in any given moment, in the end, I always felt worse.

In addition, I often ate secretly because as my weight grew, so did the judgment and scrutiny of my eating habits. This secrecy and shame about eating only amplified the emotions I felt when I ate. Tying strong emotion to food is a recipe for over- or under-eating, not for eating a healthy amount.

Because of my weight, my depression intensified. I was shamed for how I looked, how slowly I moved, what I couldn't do (or do well), the clothing size I wore (or the special store where I had to shop) and the choices I made.

While some of that shame came from other kids, it mostly came from my siblings and my father. Their styles were different, though. My siblings were basically just mean as kids can be (not necessarily intentionally or consciously), while my father — an overweight child himself and now a doctor — was tough on me about it because he was concerned for me.

My mother never really had anything to say about it either way, though she was the one buying the cookies and snacks we had on hand. I know she wanted better for me, but her motherly instinct kept her from being harsh. I do recall one specific time she actually said something to me about it. We were at a 'special' clothing store (meaning one with clothes for what was referred to as, "husky," kids back then), so it came up naturally as I struggled to button a pair of pants I was trying on. I sensed the sadness in her voice about my condition as she said she hoped I could be healthier. But that was it. Otherwise, she never outwardly judged or commented.

My weight issues were built on a foundation of depression both fueled *and* caused by emotional overeating. This was a vicious cycle in the truest sense. Contributing to this, after my parents divorced, I had to take on more adult responsibilities than a kid should. I wasn't always sure if we — or I specifically — would have the things we needed as a household. This ranged from small things such as making my own breakfast and lunch (really not a big deal, but not how it was before the divorce), to bigger things like whether our lights or telephone service would be turned off. We never went hungry, had clean clothes and a safe bed to sleep in. And there was a lot of good that came of it; for example, I learned to be much more independent and self-reliant, which is a great thing I am thankful for every day. As an adult, I know the things that did happen weren't terrible things *per se*. However, from a child's point of view, things that make you question whether you will be taken care of are very impactful on your sense-of-sense and emotional development, which can leave a lasting mark on your life[3].

Ultimately, there were consequences to the situation. The biggest result was that, in addition to depression, I became anxious that I wouldn't be all right. I questioned whether we had stability at home. Whether founded or not, I regularly felt this and consequently felt a need to step in a lot on a variety of things kids shouldn't have to step into. I felt as if things would fall apart if I was not there or doing them myself. That's a very heavy burden for a kid to bear. All the while, my weight kept increasing.

I remember being at summer camp between fifth and sixth grade when we had to get weighed for something. When I stepped on the scales, one of my counselors burst out laughing and yelled about how I weighed the same as he did despite being a foot shorter and roughly half his age. Summer camp is where I took the brunt of the cruelty outside of my home, and I hated it. While I did enjoy some aspects of camp, overall I didn't want to be there and always wished the summers away. It didn't help that the camp was very sports-focused, and I was slow and bad at sports.

One day in particular was especially hot as we were in the middle of a heat wave, and summers in New England are incredibly humid anyway. The temperature was well over 100 degrees Fahrenheit (over 38 degrees Celsius). We had an intra-camp track meet, and the counselors organizing it pitted all the fattest kids against each other in an 880-yard race (eight times around our track). The entire camp of more than 200 kids circled the track shouting and laughing while we grinded through it. It hurt physically and emotionally. I remember the pounding impact in my legs, the heavy heat of the day, the burn of the sun, the difficulty I had breathing from the thickness of the air and then very quickly the

---

[3] Pickhardt, Carl E., Ph.D., "The Impact of Divorce on Children and Adolescence." *Parenting Today* 19 Dec. 2011, http://www.doadaybook.com/divorceandkids.

feeling from my body as I began hyperventilating. I finished — not sure in what place, but very likely last — and passed out on the finish line. I awoke in the camp lake with a counselor standing over me and the camp nurse watching from the shore as they tried to get my temperature down. It was horrible, humiliating and hurtful.

Even today, as a fit adult, I still feel that anxiety before I go out on a run. It doesn't matter that I am now an experienced runner who has finished a marathon and several shorter races. The physical and emotional trauma I experienced on that track was so strong that it still makes me nervous even when I go out for a quick, easy run. I've faced what drives that anxiety, and know I can run and I will be ok. Despite my anxiety, I still get out there, and have never given in to the negative feelings and skipped a run. How I do that is a big part of what this book is about.

So what does any of this have to do with Do a Day? How will this help you achieve your goals? I share my past from my formative years so you understand where I'm coming from because if you saw me today, you might assume that I have always been fit and motivated and that I had it easy. You might think that I can't possibly understand your struggles because you think that I never struggled. You might assume that I was just born this way and that it's easy to maintain my weight and my fitness. You probably see other people on a daily basis and assume that things are easy for them, which is probably not the case. You might have thoughts in your head like, "Oh, those fit people can't possibly get it. Look at them. They don't know how hard it is or how much I hurt. They probably think I'm lazy or I don't care – but that's not true. They just don't get it." The thing is, in the same way they may not understand you, you may not understand them. I've learned this by being both 'you' and 'them'. And this applies to more than just losing weight or being fit. It applies to all aspects of our lives in which we want better for ourselves and see others who seemingly have it so easy who we think could never understand our pain or struggles.

Like so many people I imagine reading this book, I struggled. I was obese. I had tough stuff to deal with as a kid that I carried forward into my adulthood. And while I got fit before high school was over, I gained weight again as an adult and went through a second struggle with weight. I've had hard times at school, lost a job, and nearly lost my spouse to a chronic illness. While our exact situations and struggles may be different, you and I have the common bond of having these struggles, both those we've overcome and those that lie ahead. That means we can be the same in our achievement, our overcoming, and our success. Let my past be the proof to you that I'm writing this from a place of understanding of what you're going through, how it feels, how hard it is, and how strong of a person you actually are – even if you don't consciously realize that about yourself. But you will!

The title of this chapter, "Before my Dawn," means this is the background I come from before I started to Do a Day. By sharing my background with you, my hope is that you can understand how we aren't all that different. Now we can go on to Do a Day. Together.

THE END OF THE DAY

In *Day 2. Before My Dawn*, you learned about my background to understand the setting for the stories in the next chapters, but also to help illustrate some of the things kids go through that shape their adult lives. Let's look at the key messages:

- Comfort and safety are basic needs of children, and they will seek it from other sources if their family doesn't provide it, such as food or other people

- The absence of a sense of safety for a child can lead to anxiety in adults that can drive our actions and behaviors, such as fear of things going wrong if you don't step in and do them yourself, hypochondria or mistrust of others

DAY 3.
FULL OF MIND

Today, I want to teach you about mindfulness. It's a term that's used a lot these days, and it's also a central idea in the Do a Day philosophy. Understanding what mindfulness is about will help you see how to apply Do a Day to your situation so you can stay on the path to success.

According to the Merriam-Webster dictionary, mindfulness is "the practice of maintaining a nonjudgmental state of heightened or complete awareness of one's thoughts, emotions, or experiences on a moment-to-moment basis."[4] That last part about the moment-to-moment basis is the key — it's about being *in the present moment*.

A famous quotation from Buddha summarizes mindfulness perfectly. He said, "Do not dwell in the past, do not dream of the future, concentrate the mind on the present moment." Mindfulness is about being in the here and now. Not the before. Not the later.

In practical terms, it means that you don't let mistakes, failures or really *anything* from the past take away from or overpower the moment you're living right now. And it means that thoughts of the future — whether excitement, anxiety, fear, anticipation or something else — don't distract you from what's happening right now.

Let me illustrate this with some general examples, and I'll share some from my own experience later.

If you make a mistake, it is common to feel guilt, embarrassment, shame or some other bad feeling about it afterward, sometimes even after you've rectified the situation. Those negative feelings stemming from something

---

[4] Merriam-Webster
(http://www.merriam-webster.com/dictionary/mindfulness)

you can't change affect how you are *right now*. After your mistake, you start fretting about how bad everything will turn out because of what you did. So you're loaded up with shame from what you did wrong, and at the same time you are overcome or even paralyzed by fear of what will happen: getting yelled at, losing your job, going to jail, getting dumped or divorced. Whatever it is, the present moment ends up defined by feelings from the past and future.

Now let's say you need to fix a mistake you made. You cannot expect to find the best solution if you're busy beating yourself up and worrying. Sure, you could probably come up with a solution, but it is not likely to be the one that would yield the best outcome because it will be tainted by these negative feelings bookending your thought process. Mindfulness is about letting the past be the past, not focusing on what hasn't yet happened, and instead paying full attention to right now to make the best decisions and take the best actions for this very moment. Mindfulness therefore optimizes the present and then strings together a series of optimized present moments to create a better total life.

Let me share a positive example to show you that no matter how we look at the past or the present, it can keep us from being mindful. This is from the days when I first fell in love with my wife. I knew from the moment I saw her that she was "the one." I had just started business school. The day after I first really talked to her and got to know her, I was completely useless in class. My thoughts were consumed with remembering our conversation, wishing I had said this or that instead of whatever I had said, and anticipating our next conversation or what I could say or do to get her to want to go out with me. I couldn't focus in class at all, and actually have little to no memory of about two weeks of my life, because of how consumed I was with past and future interactions with this amazing woman.

Being so focused on a past experience and potential future ones cost me all my present experiences. Those present experiences also included running into her randomly during the day and not even being able to process the chance encounters, which, of course, I then obsessed about afterward with thoughts of, *Oh, man, I wish I could have just said something instead of standing there like a fool!* I may have said something, but actually was so drawn out of the "here and now" by the "before and the after" that I didn't even know if I said anything. Seriously. So my lack of mindfulness actually led to a *further* spiraling into an even *greater* lack of mindfulness. This was clearly a vicious cycle despite clearly being a very positive situation.

Let me ask you, how can you handle the present if you're overwhelmed by what was or overly focused on what will be? The answer is simply that you can't, or that you can't be focused in the way you would be if you were unencumbered by the past and future. And the cost of not being present impedes your ability to succeed.

So how does mindfulness tie into the Do a Day approach? Mindfulness is a foundational part of Do a Day. It starts with being focused on what you must handle right now and goes a step beyond simply being mindful to being focused on action. Don't worry about what you did or didn't do yesterday, and let go of concern for all you have to do from tomorrow on. Be mindful about today and today's goal. Nothing more, nothing less.

We do this by actively choosing to focus on right now. We have to be present in that decision to keep thoughts of yesterday or tomorrow from taking over. Thoughts of the past and future can drive insecurities in us around our failures or how we might fail in the future. These thoughts can spark anxiety over how we were perceived, how we will be perceived or whether we can really achieve what we're trying to achieve. We then make choices and take actions from this place of insecurity or anxiety. I say to my coaching clients and at work all the time, "When we make decisions from a place of insecurity, we make bad choices."

There are tools you can use to help you be more mindful and cut off the impact of the past or future. Some people try narrating the day in their head (e.g., "Now I'm going to get out the ingredients for dinner."). Some people meditate. The reality is, all of it is helpful, and different tools work for different people. It often takes practice, but it always means you have to consciously choose where to focus your thoughts. As I teach you about Do a Day, you will see how to do that in the various examples I share of how to apply the philosophy to the trials, tribulations and situations we all face in life. You will also see how valuable mindfulness is so you can understand that the effort it may take is worth it.

Today, you learned of the need to be present in the here and now. Tomorrow, you will learn how to Do a Day to live a healthier life.

THE END OF THE DAY

In *Day 3. Full of Mind* we learned about mindfulness, and how it ties to Do a Day. The takeaways are:

- Mindfulness is the practice of maintaining a nonjudgmental awareness of your thoughts, emotions or actions on a moment-to-moment basis

- Staying mindful means letting go of judgment of past choices, and positive or negative anticipation of what lies ahead

- Being mindful keeps us from making decisions from a place of insecurity, as we make bad choices when they are in response to our insecurities

DAY 4.
FROM "THE FAT KID" TO
"A FIT MAN"

In Day 4, I want to share my story of being overweight and getting in shape. It wasn't easy, and it wasn't linear. I struggled as many people do until I learned how to apply Do a Day to my physical struggles. I also share this story with you so you can understand that I may look fit to many, but I wasn't always that way, and that means I deeply understand the emotional, physical and social pain you can experience when you are labeled, "fat."

Before I ever did any Day, I was overweight. Strike that: I was obese. I gained ten to 20 pounds per year and hit 240 in eighth grade. I was tall, but not tall enough for that weight. My rate of weight gain slowed down as I entered high school because my height stabilized, but I still got heavier. By junior year, I was over 250. As I mentioned in *The First Step*, I remember weighing myself and seeing "248" on the scale, and then not weighing myself again for over a year. While I don't know just how heavy I got, I know that my pant size went up, so I definitely got heavier. I wore 40-inch-waist pants and would end each day with painful indent marks around my waist from how tight my pants were. I wore size 12 shoes, but fit into 10s once I lost weight. I wore XL shirts and jackets, but really should have been in XXL. I was the heaviest kid in my grade, and after a morbidly obese student graduated from high school a few years ahead of me, I was the biggest in the school by a pretty big margin.

My father rode me about it. He got me a personal trainer in middle school, which didn't do anything because mentally I wasn't ready. I wasn't ready because I was really unhappy and didn't understand why or what to do about it. While the trainer was really nice, I didn't feel a connection with him because he was this super fit guy, who was just pushing exercises on me without addressing any of the "why" behind my obesity. But how could he understand? He had no context and someone other than me hired him to get *me* into shape.

The story I kept being told by so many around me was about the totality of my obesity, and that is incredibly daunting. How much weight I had to lose, how bad it was for my health, how bad I looked, how expensive buying me clothes was becoming. I kept hearing a steady stream of the big things wrong with my big size. It was all just too much. I saw no path to addressing it because the problem was *so massive*, and the work and changes needed to solve that problem were unthinkable to a kid who had no motivation, interest or ability to work out and no emotional ability to let go of the one source of comfort he had in life — food.

My doctor told me that my ideal weight was around 170-175 pounds (roughly 77-80 kilograms) given my height and frame. Going from over 250 pounds (113 kilograms) to 175 pounds meant losing at least 75 pounds (34 kilograms), though it may have been more since I didn't know my real weight. However, while the actual number was irrelevant, the concept was daunting. If the commonly accepted weight loss trajectory was three to five pounds the first week, and then one to two pounds each subsequent week, then I was looking at what felt like an eternity of really hard work.

All I could see was a long, slow path leading up a mountain of effort to a peak topped with a big number and a lot of risks of falling along the way. But you can't climb a mountain by stepping right to the top. The only way to start climbing is to consider the different paths to the top and pick the one that most interests you and is best aligned with your abilities, then put one foot in front of the other. No matter which path you choose, you will reach the peak eventually, but only if you start walking. Once you start, the peak is irrelevant; it will be there when you get to it. In the meantime, each step is all that matters.

So how did I change my obesity situation?

I needed help in changing the story. In high school I got out of sports, which were mandatory, by getting into the Physical Education program. Being fat means you probably have knee pain, so I had a doctor's note saying I couldn't do competitive sports as a result of my bad knees. P.E. at many schools is a cop-out for non-athletic kids looking to fulfill a requirement. Not at my school — or at least that might have been the students' intention, but not their reality once they got into the program. My high school had this amazing man, Henri Andre (or "Mr. Andre," as I still call him), who takes a totally different approach to P.E. He doesn't look at it as a cop-out, whether the students do or not. He uses P.E. as an opportunity to change the mindsets of kids who may not have a positive relationship with health and exercise. He changed my life.

Mr. Andre is modest about the impact he has had on so many kids and prefers to give them full credit, but he is one of the most amazing human beings I've ever encountered, and his role in my life improvement deserves recognition. He isn't the kind of P.E. teacher who blows his whistle and yells at you to run, pick up the pace or stop slacking. He introduces you to many different ways to be active, teaches about nutrition and how biology works in relation to health, shares articles (and now TED talks and videos) that inspire and educate, and so much more. He takes a very keen interest in the wellness of his students beyond the 45 minutes he has them in class each day.

Mr. Andre never passes judgment and never talks about big, intimidating changes you need to make. Instead, he focuses on each class and each student. Sure, he has a vision for where he wants to take you, but he only talks about today. He wants each student to walk out of each session a little bit healthier and a lot wiser about not just our health, but about ourselves. He wants us to leave enlightened and inspired to want more for ourselves.

Without explicitly saying it, he showed me how to Do a Day. He was right there by my side helping me Do each Day. He would end each class by charting my accomplishment and celebrating it with me. I say, "with" and not, "for," because he didn't just score me, but made sure I felt like *I had achieved something that day.*

Mr. Andre did little things such as covering up the screen on the cardio equipment we were using so we didn't see how much time was left. He was encouraging us not to worry about what lay ahead and instead focus on the here and now. He had us lie down on a bench to do a bench press, close our eyes and visualize the weight going up, then would set the weights on the bar while our eyes were closed so we didn't have to think about just how much weight we had to lift. Instead, we would focus on successfully completing the movement. He also taught us about meditation, and had us end each session with breathing exercises meant to refocus our mind and settle our body.

Through this thoughtful, mindful approach, he slowly and steadily changed how I looked at my health and exercise. He pressed nothing upon me. He let me set my own path. Nothing happened overnight. I was in P.E. for three years before I really lost weight.

And that's what I needed; I didn't become obese quickly, so how could I become fit quickly? And how could I expect it to stick if my mind wasn't getting fit along with my body?

Mr. Andre's approach gave us the tools of wellness in a manageable way rather than ever being overbearing or daunting. In this way, we didn't feel any pressure or anxiety. We just felt that we were on a journey with a guide and a lot of self-growth. The "we" I refer to are the numerous friends I had in the class who were on similar journeys, and most of them are still fit today because we changed step by step, day by day.

And this is how fitness came to me, and why it stuck. The idea of life hacks and quick fixes is flawed. What does work is education paired with sustained, long-term effort focused on stringing together each lesson, each tool, each Day to get results — results that last.

So that's it, right?

I got fit, and stayed 100 percent fit forever, right? Well, not exactly.

The person I was in high school was a very different person from who I'd become after college, as is the case for so many of us. And I really hadn't addressed the issues I carried from childhood. I had new tools for fitness and health, but still needed to get deeper in the mental, emotional side of things. No matter how amazing Mr. Andre was, I wasn't yet at a point in my emotional maturity where I could truly face these things. That was the missing link.

So I did put on some weight, though very slowly and over several years. And I never really looked obese again. I looked American. You know the look — solid and a little meaty. I worked out, but not mindfully. I ate healthy-*ish*, but not healthily. And most importantly, I didn't address the inner me at all because of work, family and other excuses.

Fast-forwarding to 2011, my wife became very sick. We had a two-and-a-half-year-old son, and I genuinely didn't think she would live through the summer. She was sick and wasting away. She was essentially bedridden. It was scary for both of us, but also so much more profound because we had a child who was watching it happen. I was lucky enough to be able to work from home for a month to care for my wife and son while finding extra help. We also found an acupuncturist, who stopped the spiral that doctors couldn't explain, as well as a doctor who figured out what was going on.

Without going too deep into it, we found out my wife has chronic Lyme disease, which she contracted as a child. Most mainstream doctors do not accept that this is possible — they insist that you get it and either get sick or don't get sick. If you get sick, you get treated and get better, get better on your own or never get better, leading to your downfall (though I doubt they'd say this happens). Despite all the symptoms and a positive Lyme test, doctor after doctor insisted this wasn't real and maybe it was all just in her head. By "maybe," they meant "likely." Her primary care physician was content to just let her waste away to her death because there was no legitimate explanation and he was going on vacation. He said to me that he would be back in six weeks and would check in then. She was losing two pounds a day, so I asked him to do the math and realize she didn't have six weeks at this rate.

My wife is still here today and in a much better position. While her health remains a major focus of our life, we have all benefited through her illness in that we live a much healthier life.

I looked at my son and realized he was watching his mother die and his father die, only at a slower rate. And that was when I was struck with the missing link for my own lasting health. While I got fit before, the reason it didn't last in the way I wished it would is because I lacked a deep, enduring motivation. This is what I focus on first and foremost with anyone I coach — we need a true reason to pursue a goal. Being fit shouldn't be about something fleeting such as swimsuit season, a vacation, a high school reunion or a wedding. Once those temporal things pass, why are you trying to be fit? You lose your reason and then you lose your fitness.

For me, my motivation before was to not be obese and to be seen as something other than "the fat kid" in people's eyes. Well, once I got fit and went to college where no one knew me as anything but fit, I had reached my goal. So the pressure came off, but more importantly, the reason for being fit stopped existing. And my goal was still met — no one ever looked at me that way again even when I gained some of the weight back, because I just looked like everyone else. I didn't look bigger than most people, so I didn't stand out for the wrong reason.

That wasn't an enduring motivator, but more importantly, it wasn't profound or deep within me. It depended on the judgment of others. I needed to find something much bigger and deeper than that.

So my goal, my reason for being healthy was clear and massive — I needed to be there for my son and be a positive, inspiring role model around how to live life.

Being overweight and unhappy is not inspiring or positive. I needed a change. I knew this was the right goal because the day after this hit me, my life changed completely. It was like a light switch that was turned on the evening of June 30th, 2011. I will never forget it. July 1st, 2011, my workout felt totally different. I woke up driven. I engaged in my exercise with purpose. I created structure around my workouts. I started newbodi.es. Literally in one day. And it's stuck since then. Literally every Day has been Done. My weight has been consistent, my health has been strong, and my son makes healthy choices for himself without being told to. I can honestly say he's proud of me and appreciates my health and what it means for him. I know because we talk about it, and I see it in his eyes.

I love this one story that really illustrates the impact my path has had on my son. He and I went to meet my father for lunch at a restaurant. My son was three (a year after my light-switch moment). My dad got a pepperoni pizza that honestly looked horrible. The plate it was on had a slight bowl shape about it, so the middle of the pizza became a collection area for this disgusting pool of orange oil from the cheese and pepperoni. The story played out like this:

My son:	"Grandpa, is that pepperoni on your pizza?"
My father:	"Yes, it is. Would you like a piece?"
My son:	"Oh, no, I'd never eat that."
My father:	"You're too restrictive with him." (looking at me with a scowl)
Me:	"I didn't say anything, Dad. He came up with that on his own."

I was so proud of my little guy for his awareness of choices like this, but also because I had never talked to him about this. In fact, my wife had talked about how some pepperoni can be bad for you, but there are also healthier pepperoni without nitrates and higher-quality meat, which he had even eaten. It's not like he thought all pepperoni was unhealthy, or like he'd never had it before. He had no way to know which kind this was, but was choosing not to take a chance either way and recognizing how the disgusting way this bright-orange-oil-slick pizza sat on the plate was a sign that it wasn't a healthy choice.

That was the proof that I was on the right path. Not that someone thought I looked good, or that a scale said one number or another. That stuff is ultimately meaningless. No, a much bigger thing in this universe was driving me and it was on the right path. And my son isn't going anywhere, so him being a key driving force in my health is going to endure. Every day. And that's why I know I will Do health today. And tomorrow, I will Do another Day.

In section II (*The "Why" & "What" to Do: Motivation & Goals*), we will set you up to find your real motivation and then build goals that will lead you to success. Those are the building blocks, and Do a Day is the way you execute.

Now that you've seen my transformative Day, let's look at the next Day, which is how to Do a Day as a parent.

THE END OF THE DAY

Day 4. From "The Fat Kid" to "A Fit Man" shared how Do a Day can help with the struggle so many people have with their weight and fitness. Do a Day is critical in weight-loss struggles because:

- Overcoming obesity can seem impossibly large when looking at it in totality

- Using Do a Day, you can make choices today to contribute to the overall weight loss and fitness level you aspire to achieve

- To keep the weight off takes a life full of a Do a Day approach built on a deep, enduring underlying motivation

DAY 5.
A DAY OF PARENTING

Today, I want to show how Do a Day ties to parenting — something that's amazing and rewarding, and also hard. The work it requires, the shift in focus from your life to the life you created, and the gravity of the responsibility can be too much if you look at it all at once. Using Do a Day, you can raise well-adjusted, happy, healthy kids who become well-adjusted, happy, healthy adults.

I'm a dad. It's my greatest achievement. My pride in my son and in being his father are beyond words. Being a parent is also one of the scariest and hardest things you can do, whether you're in the role of dad or mom, biologically or by some other means. Parenting is hard work, and the ramifications are huge. You're creating and crafting a human life. That life will be out in the world and needs to be able to fend for itself, and then will likely be responsible for creating and shaping other human lives. That's a massive burden when you think about the generations you're ultimately responsible for.

For any parents out there, you know the feeling of sleep deprivation. It's that thing everyone warned you about, and you thought you understood and figured it would be hard. Then you lived it, and you realized there is no understanding it until you live it. That's a tremendously hard thing to go through, and the end never feels like it's in sight.

Then there are days when your child is so sick, or is bullied or made fun of, and there's nothing you can do to take that away or make it so it never happened. You can comfort them and help them through it, but you can't undo it. You can't protect them from every negative experience they will have, and that hurts so deeply and can be daunting.

And then there are all the milestones they'll pass, and the amazing feelings you'll get watching this all happen mixed with the sense of loss as they grow farther away from being your little baby. You can't hold them in your arms because they don't fit in there anymore. They don't need you to snuggle them up so they can fall asleep. They grow up, and they grow independent, and that is a lot to take as a parent. It's beautiful to watch and fills you with pride, but it's still a lot to take.

Watching this happen and thinking about the potentiality of it all — all the pain they may experience, how they'll pull away, how you won't get more than 15 minutes of sleep at any given time for weeks to come, how your parenting mistakes could ruin them and generations to come (wow, talk about something to feel pressure about!) — is crushing. It's heartbreaking and scary.

If you look at it this way, you can easily become consumed with anxiety, fear and sadness. What you don't do is live present in the moment with your child and enjoy what you do have with them right then and right there. You may not give them what they need because you're overwhelmed by the bigness of it all.

I remember when my son was eating an ice cream cone, and part of the cone got stuck in his throat, and he started choking. The idea of your child not breathing, then turning blue from lack of oxygen, and then going unconscious and potentially dying strikes you. Can you help them? Can you get an ambulance there fast enough?

Well, let me tell you firsthand, you can't do any of that if you stand there focusing on the totality of your child choking to death.

My wife called 911 as I helped my son, trying to dislodge the piece of cone. We acted fast and specifically on the immediate steps we needed to act on to save him. The ambulance came in about two minutes, but he was already fine by then and was just interested in the ambulance and meeting the paramedics who came out from inside it.

This is one example and not a series of steps that work toward a goal of creating a really well-rounded, happy, healthy, good person. But more than just being a specific example, it is also part of a series of things that we do around good and bad situations as parents. We couldn't do any of these things if we stopped and stared at the implications of each situation.

Yes, you are responsible for so much as a parent. But remember, life is a series of Days. You have to Do each one while being present in the demands of that Day. Do each as best you can, and you will naturally end up adding up to a complete and wonderful life for one of the most important things in *your* life.

Tomorrow, we start marathon training. Let's go Do it.

THE END OF THE DAY

Day 5. A Day of Parenting shows how Do a Day can apply to raising children to become well-adjusted, capable adults. The key messages are:

- Parenting comes with great responsibilities and demands that can feel overwhelming at times

- You aren't raising a child from birth to independent-adulthood all at once

- Using Do a Day, you can make choices each day to handle the responsibility of parenthood and raise your kids into amazing adults

DAY 6.
MY 725 MILE MARATHON

In this chapter, I want to frame a physical goal many people have through the lens of Do a Day. Completing a marathon is a goal I never had for most of my life as it was just too far-fetched and impossible to even consider. When you don't run, the idea of running that far is a non-starter. There's a reason why there are training plans for first-time runners — it *is* possible. Through Do a Day, you will see how to achieve a huge physical feat like the marathon by training each day for that day. Over the course of time, the miles add up, and you become a marathoner.

If marathons are 26.2 miles long, why did I title this chapter *My 725 Mile Marathon*? That was roughly the total mileage in my five-month journey of marathon training. I can't imagine most people would look at the idea of running 725 miles without having at least a little bit of trepidation and hesitation. Even famous ultramarathon runners like Dean Karnazes and Scott Jurek would probably think twice before setting out for that kind of distance.

But marathon training isn't done in a single run. My training plan was spread over 24 weeks, which is an unusually long time. Usually marathon training plans are more like 16 to 20 weeks long. I had the time to train, and wanted to ensure I built my capabilities smoothly and steadily to lower the risk of injury from overtraining or ramping up too quickly. That additional time meant that my training plan was longer than most — 725 miles for me rather than the roughly 650 miles in a typical first-time marathon training plan.

Before beginning training for the marathon, I had not run farther than 13.1 miles, which I did twice in half-marathon races. After both races, I took several months off to recover from injuries. In my marathon training plan, my longest run would be 20 miles (excluding the actual marathon), and there were plenty of days with solid distance and speed in the same run. To say it was going to be a piece of cake would be unfair. But to say it was undoable was equally unfair.

So how could I possibly run 725 miles, do speed work and not get injured? Injury aside, how could I even run so much in the first place?

Simple. I did it through Do a Day. That is, I got up each day, looked at my training plan for *that* day, and committed to Do a Day. I didn't look at what I had to do weeks later because those distances weren't part of my set of capabilities on that day. To judge them off today's capabilities as too far, too hard or just generally too demanding and frightening was unfair and irrational. The time to evaluate their doability[5] would be when I was heading out the door to do each one. By Doing a series of Days between today and that milestone date far off at the end of my training, I would be adding up my capabilities to conquer that final marathon distance.

That isn't to say I wasn't aware of what I had to do over the course of the training. I knew the ultimate distance and had a sense of what each week looked like. My weeks followed similar patterns of what types of workouts happened on which days, so I always had an idea that my "hard" day was coming up, or that I'd have real distance to cover a few days from now. You don't turn off your ability to know what the future will hold, and that's okay. This isn't about ignoring reality, fooling yourself or denying the truth. It's about not *over*-focusing on what is to come by instead spending your full focus on today.

Let's just do a little mental exercise for a moment. My long runs were on Fridays. If every Monday, when each training week started, I got overcome with anxiety about the

---

[5] It's a word, trust me. OK, it isn't a word, but it should be. And you should still trust me.

upcoming long run five days away, it would impact my performance on my runs between now and then. Why? Well, the mind is good at protecting the body. If it knows there's a big effort coming, it will restrict performance to ensure you have reserves for the big push.[6] That's one downside to focusing on the long run. But the other downside is that doing so ignores the fact that I have a recovery day (a day with a lighter workout that excludes any running whatsoever) between now and then, two of my favorite workouts (strides[7]), and a complete rest day the day after the long run (followed by yet *another* recovery day). So why is it okay to just focus on the "bad" in store? There's reward baked in, too (the reality is, I generally really liked my long runs. In fact, only two of them were negative experiences for me, if you can even call them that).

Now let's look at the implications of just focusing on the "reward" of rest. If I focused on that, I might push myself too hard in workouts leading up to it and go beyond what I'm supposed to be doing at this point in my training. That is when injury occurs. I might be so focused on the rest day that I end up bagging my workout early because future rest becomes the focus, so I'd cut short this Day to Do the next. You know the feeling — if you're running to some end

---

[6] There's a lot of research that proves this. An interesting piece Alex Hutchinson of Runner's World wrote about shows the effect with VO_2 Max — the maximum volume of oxygen our bodies can process at a time. Read it here: http://sweatscience.com/when-is-vo2max-not-max/. And another cool one by Alex on the finishing kick being in your head: http://sweatscience.com/the-finishing-kick-is-in-your-head-not-your-legs/.

[7] Strides are when you pick up the pace to 90 percent to 95 percent of your maximum sprinting effort for a short period of time by starting at an easy pace, and then ramping up to and back down from that high effort. These are typically done as intervals after a run. My stride workout was generally a four-mile run followed by four stride repetitions of a tenth of a mile strides followed by quarter-mile recovery jogs. The total run came to about 5.25 miles. And I came to love them.

point, do you run *through* the finish line or do you slow down just before it? Thinking about the part after the finish line can mean you mentally move the finish line sooner in your mind, and don't put in what you're supposed to.

Focusing on the hard steps out in the future that you may not currently be able to tackle, but will be when you get to them, causes unnecessary mental duress and potentially poor performance as the mind protects your reserves. Focusing on the easy stuff that comes after the tougher stuff can also lead to problems today. Whether looking at a hard or easy time to come tomorrow, putting your mind on tomorrow instead of today means you're living today by tomorrow's rules. And that costs you. In this Day, we focus on this Day, and we Do that.

This holds for the past, too. I had gotten injured after getting back on the road too soon after taking a bad fall in a trail race (discussed more in *Having a Bad Day*). Because I was so concerned with being able to deliver on the rest of my training, I didn't take an extra day or two to recover. Instead, I pushed through a tough workout and ended up with a tear in my calf that stopped me cold. I was grateful to employ a number of recovery methods and get back to training after about a week of complete rest (and easing back into it very slowly), but every time I did that type of workout (called a tempo run), I got nervous. Every time I ran in that same location, I got nervous, which was a problem because it was close to my house, so it was a frequent part of most runs I did. And every time I ran in that spot during a tempo run, I was nearly overcome by my anxiety.

I got through it by altering my route a bit, which I needed to do anyway to keep things interesting. I also sat down and wrote about it. Through writing, I expressed what I was feeling under the surface that drove my choices. Through that expression, I exposed where I was going wrong and could see what I needed to do differently. I also allowed myself to get it all out there rather than having it fester under the surface. I realized that I wasn't following Do a Day in this situation. It didn't take much self-discovery to see that I was giving in to anxiety and letting that define this aspect of my life. Worst of all, I know better. As Oprah says, "When we know better, we do better." So I did.

I have tools at my disposal to help, as we all do. The first and most important is to get the feelings and thoughts out and work with them. I blogged about my injury in the race and my subsequent poor choice about not taking enough time off and how that all played out. I faced what happened, how my choices played into it and how I could have avoided it. I openly discussed how I had given in to being controlled rather than controlling things myself. Getting those words out allowed me to be past it. I confined it to something that *had* happened rather than being something that *was* happening. It was yesterday. Now is today. They aren't the same. This is mindfulness in action, and it took some conscious work on my part to make it that way.

The answer is to be aware of what lies ahead, but leave it there. Don't deny the events of the past or create an alternate reality where they didn't happen, but let them be part of the past and nothing more. Bring the mind back to today, focus on it, deliver it without concern for tomorrow or yesterday.

While it is fair to say that I'm a marathoner, that doesn't tell you about how it went. In a nutshell, it didn't go nearly as well as I'd have hoped it would. Since it was my first marathon, understandably I had nervousness and excitement in spades. I was also out of town and don't usually sleep well in hotels, plus I changed hotels before the race, so I only got one night in each, adding disruption into the mix. That meant I slept a total of about three hours over the two nights before the marathon. Lastly, I think I picked up a stomach bug. For those who don't know, your stomach usually has issues during endurance events as the body diverts blood flow to the muscles, thus suspending or at least slowing digestion. This can cause gastric distress, and would amplify the severity of any stomach bug I had caught.

I started the race feeling good. I was so happy and excited. I was in Chicago, which is an amazing city. The weather was gorgeous, if a little warm for a fall marathon, but it meant the crowds were huge. I covered the first three miles around the pacing I wanted to hit them at, and was doing a good job controlling myself from going out too quickly — the number one mistake first-timers make.

As the miles ticked by, I was very much in the "today" of it. I wasn't thinking about days past, nor was I even thinking about the miles that still lay far ahead. I was doing a good job of mentally focusing on the current mile. At the same time, I was feeling tired and didn't have a good feel for the energy in my body. I'm typically very in tune with that, especially after becoming vegan (as I'll discuss in the next chapter, *A Veggie a Day*). My diet was a bit off while on the road since I didn't have a kitchen, but I thought I had done a pretty good job of meeting my needs without adding anything I wasn't used to. And I usually need to get past the 5K mark before I start to feel good on a run.[8] So, like figuring out if my stomach issues were from illness or not, I wasn't sure that there was a problem here, or just the normal feeling as I got fully warmed up.

Getting to seven miles is often when I feel my best on any run, but that was not the case on this day. I kept waiting to break out of my "warm up" funk. I ate some of my energy chews while sipping some of my electrolyte mixture. They didn't do anything for my energy levels. Miles eight and nine seemed to take forever to come, and of course I wasn't even halfway through the race. I felt like I

---

[8] This is a biological thing rather than mental. The body changes how it makes energy after 20-25 minutes of aerobic exercise (the duration can vary from person to person and your level of training). I usually feel like I can just keep running after I cross that 5K mark, whereas it feels like a real chore to break 5K.

needed to just get to the half-marathon mark and stop judging how it was going until then. I knew that volunteers from the charity I was running for, St. Jude's Children's Research Hospital, would be in the cheering section just a little after the halfway point, and that would give me a huge boost.

The half-marathon mark came and went, and I knew I was in trouble. I did get a boost as I passed the charity cheering section, but it was very short-lived. I decided — very unwisely — to break my personal conviction not to make any newbie mistakes and use something I had not trained with. At the hydration station, I got a cup of Gatorade. After finishing it, I got another. I hadn't had Gatorade since December 2004, which was nearly 11 years earlier. I might have been tired before, but what was about to happen was much worse.

As I approached the 16-mile mark, I still didn't feel lifted, so I decided I'd try taking a bathroom break to see if it helped. It made me more comfortable, but I was still tired. I got some water, and went to start running again. I was hit with the most intense stomach pain I have felt in a very long time (if not in my entire life), and I've had Salmonella twice. It stopped me dead in my tracks. I pushed myself to make that just a second-long pause, and get back to at least walking. Just before mile 17, I told myself I have to try to jog again, and I did. The pain was not quite as severe, but was still bad, making it hard to get my body moving.

I eyed the medical tent at the mile marker and wondered if I was foolish for not heading straight there. Instead, I got a cup of water, and walked while I sipped it. That went on for about a half-mile, and then I tried to run again. The pain was a little better, but still tough to bear, and I was incredibly tired. I walked to the 18-mile marker, and still couldn't run or jog. I eyed the medical tent there, but decided I needed to try to push on for the next mile since the intensity was dying down a bit.

When walking, I got a pat on the back from a guy who saw the struggle in me, and knew I needed the emotional and mental support of someone who got it. As he went ahead, I decided I could do this, and try to run again. As I pushed, I found him walking just up ahead, and returned the favor.

As I came to the water station at the 19-mile marker, I walked again. That guy caught up to me, and we walked together for a bit, sharing our stories. Turns out he is a preacher named Tyler who has had an inspiring life. I credit that short personal connection for getting me through the pain and exhaustion.

I kept at it for the next few miles, with my walk breaks getting a little shorter each time, and finally ending completely by the 24-mile marker, meaning I had 2.2 miles to go. Thing is, I was not thinking straight, and thought it meant I was *starting* my 24th mile rather than the 25th. That is, I only had 1.2 miles to go. I would have run from the 23rd if I were thinking more clearly.

I caught up with another St. Jude's Hero, as we were called on the team, whom I had talked to on the way to the start, and we ran together to the 1,000 meters sign, meaning there was 1 kilometer to go. The markers were there every 200 meters or so. They flew by, yet also felt like they took forever — kind of hard to explain the feeling, but I was thankful for each one.

I was upset that things had gone the way they had gone. I was aiming to finish in less than four hours, and I was now at about 4:40. Five months of training were being thrown away because of two bad nights of sleep and stomach pain.

I could have gone down such a dark spiral. I wasn't happy about the situation, but let's get some perspective here. There's no way I could even have gotten as far as I did before walking without that training. There's no question in my mind that I couldn't have gotten through such a grueling experience without all that training. I was in fantastic shape and was able to endure because I had put in the work.

If I felt like everything was ruined and thrown away, I could have just dropped out and gotten a DNF (Did Not Finish) as my time. I could have been labeled as a failure (at least in my mind). I would have had to explain to all the people who supported me, to my wife and son, to myself why I didn't make it. I could have thrown away Today because it didn't measure up to five months of Yesterdays. Or I could get back into Today. I could tell that my stomach had stabilized a lot. My energy was low physically, but very high mentally as I was so close to the end, and had these personal connections boosting me.

I made Today my priority, and performed for Today relative to Today only. What I did before didn't matter. What I might do again was irrelevant (and honestly, Tomorrow wasn't anywhere on my mind). I singularly focused on the distance between me and a marathon finisher's medal. In fact, I didn't even care about the time. I didn't know what it would be anymore, unlike when I was obsessing over it earlier in the race when sub-four was possible, and then when it had slipped away and I just tried to do a lot of math with my tired brain to keep me going.

Do a Day. Get those feet moving. Unlock those locked-up hips and make those legs turn over. Beat those blisters on my toes. Pump those arms. Breathe. Do a marathon on this Day.

I can say very clearly today that the marathon didn't go how I wanted it to, but I finished, and I'll be damned if I am not very proud of the way I beat that last mile, and especially the last 1,000 meters. I finished in a way worthy of every run I put in over those five months, and really worthy of every run I've put in since I started running in 2012. I finished strong, fast, proud and triumphant. The only reason I did that is because I made that finish my Day. And I did it.

My final time was 4:44:28.

Do I wish it were faster? Let me answer that a different way — it will be better in my next marathon.

One of the reasons I know I will have my second chance is that I eat in a way that fuels my body healthily and allows me to achieve physically. Let's Do a Day of eating better.

THE END OF THE DAY

Day 6. My 725 Mile Marathon shares my marathon story to show how Do a Day can break down a huge goal into pieces and work through the trials and tribulations that come along the way. Remember:

- Big physical goals like running a marathon lend themselves well to Do a Day because you *have* to break them into pieces for training

- Despite a training plan breaking down the total into digestible parts, you have to actively focus on your plan for the day to mindfully avoid the gravity of the total

- Do a Day is crucial to making smart choices each day, rather than those based on past problems or future pressures, and will lead to a better outcome

DAY 7.
A VEGGIE A DAY

Like exercising regularly, changing your eating habits is another "impossible" thing many of us think we should do. I have tried to follow several diets through my attempts to lose weight, and in this chapter I share how I have adopted and stuck to the most extreme approach to eating I've ever tried, and have actually found it to be easy through applying Do a Day to what I eat, every day, so that you can see how you can do the same regardless of what kind of eating choices you might be best off making.

I'm a vegan. Well, let me rephrase that. I'm *plant powered*. What's the difference? Well, not much, except the word "vegan" tends to evoke the notion that you're about to get lectured about your decision to eat animal products or how you're single-handedly destroying the Earth. That's not how I roll — I'd love for others to give it a try and to reap the benefits for themselves and the planet, but I'm not the preachy-judgy type. I'm in it for my own health, so it wouldn't be right for me to come down on someone else for their choices, when my reasons are personal. I feel I've made the right decision for me, and it may be right for others, but that's not my call to make.

Before I go further, let me educate those who don't know what vegan means. Diet exists on a spectrum from omnivores (people who eat everything) to people who eat only certain things (or *don't* eat certain things). The first stop on this spectrum is those who don't eat red meat (or pork). You'll also hear about people following a Paleo diet (from the word *Paleolithic*). The idea is to eat as our cave-dwelling ancestors ate, which means no processed foods, no grain (so it is also a gluten-free diet) and no dairy, leading to a diet that includes meat but is heavy in veggies and preferential to raw foods (there's debate about the last part).

A common step toward vegetarian or vegan eating is what is called, "pescatarian." I'll admit, when I first heard it I thought that was a religion, like Episcopalian or Presbyterian or something. But it means you eat a vegetable-based diet but will also eat fish (some pescatarians also eat dairy and/or eggs). A pescatarian is a vegetarian who eats seafood.

A vegetarian is someone who does not eat meat. That is, they eat plants but many will also eat eggs, honey and dairy (aka "animal products"). Sometimes you'll hear the term "lacto-ovo," meaning dairy and eggs, respectively. Some vegetarians will nix either the lacto or the ovo. If you drop them both, then you're basically talking about being vegan (honey being the other item to drop). That is, you eat a fully plant-based diet with no animal products whatsoever. If it comes from an animal or is made by animals directly or indirectly, it's out. That includes honey, since bees produce it from their bodies. True vegans will also not wear animal-based clothing, like leather, suede and silk.

To most people, a discussion like this sounds horribly restrictive, and leads to all the comments about what they can't give up or how they could never do it. My consistent response is somewhat meant to be funny but also serious and true. I simply say, "Well, not with that attitude, you can't."

The thing is, I sort of had that attitude, too. I wasn't quite so bad, but I did look at a few key things that I felt were crucial components of my healthy diet, and I wasn't sure if I *could* give them up or how I *would* give them up. Not that I couldn't do it *emotionally*, but more logistically. I also wasn't sure that there was a benefit to giving them up, and thought there might even be a health cost. My thinking was focused on things like, without eggs, how could I get enough protein before my heavy morning workouts?

So how *did* I become vegan? You guessed it. I chose to Do a Day. I came to that decision while reading Rich Roll's amazing autobiography, *Finding Ultra*. If you don't know who Rich is, Google him. If you do know who he is but haven't read his book, you absolutely must read it. If you've read it and haven't listened to his podcast, subscribe. To find links to everything Rich Roll, just visit www.newbodi.es/richroll. In a nutshell, Rich is an ultra-endurance athlete (a triathlete, specifically) who is also a vegan and is committed to helping others live life as the best possible version of themselves. In short, he's an inspiring guy.

I had read a few other books by vegans, including *Eat & Run* by ultra-runner Scott Jurek. It's a great piece that tells the story of his life intermixed with recipes for vegan eating. One key goal of the book is to educate you on how to go vegan while inspiring you to try it. I thoroughly enjoyed the book and was inspired by Scott's life, but didn't feel the draw to go vegan. I maybe had a curiosity and interest in some of the recipes (I developed a chili recipe inspired by his that you can find at www.newbodi.es/chili), but nothing struck me hard enough to make me decide not to eat animal products.

Rich's story is one of transformation from alcoholism and weight problems to going vegan and being named one of the fittest men alive (not to mention doing several double Ironman races — aka Ultraman — and being one of the first two people to do EPIC5, which is five Ironman-distance triathlons on five Hawaiian islands in a week or less). There's something in how Rich shares his evolution, talks about making the change in diet and in life, and then challenges you to give a real reason not to join in. He calls you out right there as you read the book, and I couldn't help but feel compelled to at least give it a try.

So instead of focusing on all the things I couldn't eat ever again; how hard it would be to make it work; all the family functions I'd have to work around or look weird at; the business travel I would be stuck without food on; having to ditch the eggs that had become so integral to my morning workouts; and on and on, I just said out loud, "Yeah, I can Do a Day. I'll do it tomorrow." Make no mistake — that

"I'll do it tomorrow" wasn't me putting it off; that was a line in the sand I was drawing and setting a firm schedule. It was around 8:30 at night, so there was no time left in the day to sweat it. I hung out with my wife, went to bed without discussing it and that was it.

That was the first time I used the phrase, "Do a Day." I put no planning into it. I decided I'd lay aside my concerns for the future, and focus on making tomorrow work.

So how was my day?

It went shockingly well. That first day was so much easier than I had told myself going vegan could be. Why? Simple — I didn't make it bigger than it really was. By constraining it to a short, specific goal, I knew I could get through it, so I went for it. By removing the overbearing, crushing idea of forever, I was able to go into it with a lighter, more positive attitude, which allowed me to enjoy it and see the possibilities rather than the restrictions.

That first day was easy — easier than how I was eating before had been. Since I don't eat many processed or prepackaged foods, I found it was simple to know if something was vegan or not. Think about it: You can easily tell if there's a hunk of steak in your food if it isn't ground up, made into a single color, coated in some sweet coating and then wrapped in some packaging. I had been eating healthily for four years by avoiding added sugar, dairy and other items, including fruit, beets, corn and carrots because of their high natural sugar levels. I found that I constantly had to scrutinize labels, and it often wasn't until I had gotten through to the end of the ingredient list that I'd find something I couldn't eat as an ingredient, or I'd look at something "healthy" and see that the sugar or non-fiber carbs (total carbs minus fiber carbs) were too high, and have to avoid it.

Since I'd gone vegan, if it didn't have animal products in it, I could just eat it. Done. Want an apple? Eat an apple. I hadn't eaten an apple without guilt or a sense of breaking the rules in four years. An apple! Seriously. That one day I did felt so free. I was happy and saw myself doing another day just like that. So I did.

That was two days. You may be wondering if I did a third, or if I'm still doing it. I'm proud and happy to say that I am, and just passed the two-year mark as I wrote this. Now, I will say that I have not been 100 percent vegan 100 percent of the time. I have probably been 100 percent vegan 95 percent of the time. That is, I have allowed myself in certain special occasions to relax slightly. Those occasions have been focused on my family: sharing an ice cream with my son, or celebrating his birthday with a piece of cake that has eggs and milk in it. But there are stretches of weeks and weeks where I am purely vegan. I don't want to say "strict" because that's the wrong idea — it's not strict. I'm happy to do it. I'm not constrained. I'm doing something great for myself that happens to have a lot of benefits for others by doing my part to create slightly less demand for animal meat and other animal products and to reduce the impact on our planet.

And those times I have slipped could have resulted in me throwing in the towel on being vegan, but because I looked at them as isolated actions on isolated days, they had no impact on my choices the next day. I'm certain the reason I have stuck with it is because I have removed all the pressure of words like "forever" and "never" from the equation. I always felt pressure around what I did and didn't eat, so when I'd make a bad choice, it would come with guilt and negativity and feelings of failure. Isolating things to one day has kept that guilt and negativity from creeping in.

Sticking with this vegan diet has given me some health benefits. First, my cholesterol levels are outstanding. My LDL (the bad cholesterol) level is half of what my doctor says is normal for someone my age. My resting heart rate is in the 40s. That's a function of my fitness, but also from the fact that my arteries are free from any plaque. And lastly, my marathon training showed me how much more quickly I recover from injury (whether a specific injury or the general trauma the body experiences from tough workouts).

Despite people warning me that I couldn't possibly train for or finish a marathon without meat and dairy (specifically for the dairy protein), I did all of that, and was shockingly free of major injuries — even when I got hurt, I got back to it more quickly than I would have other times in my life. And lastly, having battled weight issues much of my life, I will say I've never had an easier time managing my weight than since I went vegan. It doesn't matter how much I eat or what I eat within this whole food, plant-based diet that I live — my weight stays very consistent, as does my body fat.

These are the reasons I chose to Do this Day, so it's fantastic how well being vegan has delivered. That success of the Do a Day approach showed me so clearly how much it can make for a better life, including the work aspect of our lives — however the word "work" is defined in each of our lives. We spend so much of our time working that we need a way to be better at it and ensure it doesn't take our life force from us. Do a Day is that way — let's go learn how.

THE END OF THE DAY

Day 7. A Veggie a Day uses my extreme example to show how you can make major shifts in Diet through Do a Day and reap the benefits for your life.

- Changes in eating can seem daunting and restrictive regardless of how extreme the changes are or aren't

- Following the Do a Day approach allows you to confine food choices to a single day, and avoid the pressure of restrictions

- Do a Day frees us from the guilt and judgment of bad choices we've made or might make, and allows us to get back to and stay on the right path instead of quitting because of a misstep

- Stringing together a series of right choices with Diet can yield meaningful improvements in your health and your life overall

DAY 8.
DO A DAY AT THE OFFICE

In this chapter, I will take you through several examples of how Do a Day can get you through the tough challenges people face daily at work, from issues with your boss or a coworker to times when you may make a major mistake that you fear could cost you your job. By following the Do a Day approach, you can get through these situations while ensuring you aren't the cause of your own downfall.

Work. We all do it in one way, shape or form. Whether it's for ourselves, for others, for a business, for a non-profit, for the government or for something else entirely, we all do *something* with our time that isn't sitting around relaxing. Some of us must work to make ends meet; some of us work as full-time parents to raise our children; and some of us work because we love our job.

Work, as with pretty much every other part of our lives, has ups and downs. We have good days and bad days. We have tough bosses, employees, clients and peers, and we have things we *must* do that aren't necessarily the things we *want* to do (e.g., paperwork, bookkeeping, laundry, audits, manual labor or getting thrown up on by a sick child). In other words, even the best, most rewarding work has tough moments that we must go through as we reach for a higher level of achievement.

As with everything else I have tackled, the way to get through these tough moments is to deal with them in the day they come up and keep them there. Go to bed and wake up the next day without them. Don't let them spill into the entire future of that job, worrying about whether things will work out or if what lies ahead will be something you can handle.

Earlier in my career, when I was a management consultant, I had built an involved, elaborate Excel model of a massive operation. My client had made a series of acquisitions and was in the process of making their latest one. While they had acquired many companies, they had integrated none. This time was to be different: After this acquisition, the client was going to integrate their operations into a coordinated, cohesive national unit. They had over 2,000 employees in this division, 20-plus offices of various sizes and eight large service centers all spread across the country. While there were more employees than needed, they wanted to keep many of them, which meant the new operation needed to be mindful of where people were based today and where they would be needed tomorrow. It was complicated. Oh, and by the way, the whole thing was mission critical; their $6 billion business could not break down during the reorganization. To use an analogy I've heard several other times, it was like trying to change the engine on a plane … while flying.

I worked for three months, putting in many 70-plus-hour weeks, and working at least six days a week with no vacation (let alone any semblance of weekends). Luckily, my wife worked for the same consulting company, so she understood more than I think any spouse should be expected to understand.

Despite the grueling work schedule and frantic pace, I loved it. I was doing difficult and inspiring work that would have a huge impact, and the results would be very tangible (a rarity for management consulting work). I got huge sets of data on every transaction that had been handled in the previous year to project what would be needed for staffing going forward. Using that volume, I designed the new organization, a transition plan to get there from where they were today (including details such as what would happen to each employee, what costs were involved, and any relocation or early retirement offers needed). I presented the work to the head of the business, who was impressed and appreciative. I went around the country to help spread the plan and share it with local leadership. And then I moved on and did a different project.

Then one day about three weeks into my new project, I got a phone call from one of my day-to-day contacts at the client. I had made a material mistake in my work. That huge dataset on which I based everything had a blank row in it under which the data continued. But I hadn't noticed that there was more data after the break. I had omitted that data from my model; I didn't account for about 12 percent of the actual volume that was flowing through the operation. Once I was made aware of this and brought in the additional data, the impact was meaningful: There would be changes in which offices closed or not, who would be needed where, and the total cost and ultimate cost savings of the operation and transition. The net result was still very good for the organization, but the mistake was very public and sloppy, so I looked bad.

I felt horrible. I was embarrassed, nervous, ashamed and sick to my stomach. And those feelings weren't present just on that day I found out what I had done wrong. I felt that way for a good month, which was four times longer than the time needed to fix the mistake, take responsibility to the client, explain to others in the firm what had happened, and ultimately not to hear another word about it from anyone. After about a week, the world moved on. But I didn't. I punished myself much longer than anyone else did, and not in a minor way. It impacted my work on my new project, it impacted my interactions at work and in my personal life, and it impacted my mental and physical health. I doubted myself all the time. I had been about to get promoted, so while I was certain that was out the window, I was also pretty sure I'd actually get fired.

My appraisal came, and there was literally no mention of this mistake at all. Not a word was written, not a score was impacted (we were rated on a five-point scale on a number of measures, including things like the accuracy and quality of our work). What did come up was my attitude and interactions in the past month — the time just after the incident leading up to my performance review. The actual mistake wasn't an issue, but the way I let it spill into not just the relevant days, but into every day after that and impact how I did everything was where people took issue with my performance — rightfully so.

It's easy to sit here a decade later and say that I should have just let it go and moved on. I recognize that during that period, though, it wasn't easy. Or, more accurately, when you don't live your life with a Do a Day approach overall, it isn't easy. However, when you allow bad things to happen only within the context in which they exist, and you actively think about whether you're letting them spill over into more time and aspects of your life than they deserve, and then you make a conscious choice to contain them to their respective Day, it *becomes* easy.

It may take practice, but it will get easier each time, and when you see how bad things and tough times are contained and don't ruin the rest of your life or career, you reinforce to yourself that it is right to confine these events to their respective Day. It is all right to allow yourself to be okay tomorrow. That doesn't mean you ignore what happened, or create an alternative reality where they didn't happen or don't matter at all. It just means you keep things in perspective instead of catastrophizing and expanding the scope of the issue.

Since the example I shared, I've had other tough days at work. I've had unstable and manipulative bosses, difficult coworkers, tough clients, dishonest business partners and more. I've been on the losing end of a political battle amongst people above me that resulted in my leaving a company I thought I'd be at until retirement. And aside from all these outside forces for difficulties in work, I've made many mistakes where the blame sits squarely with me. Yet I've also had a great career filled with many successes. And that is true for my home life: lots of tough times, lots of great times, and overall things move forward and life is good.

I've made missteps as a husband and a father, raising my voice, being outwardly frustrated or saying things I wish I hadn't. I've felt like a failure in both roles at times. But it's more accurate to say I failed in a moment or situation. Despite any individual failure, *I* am not a failure.

I had a chance to test my ability to apply Do a Day in a work situation where I had made a mistake. We often hear that two things we should never talk about at work are politics and religion. Luckily, I only talked about one of them in this example at a work dinner I attended. I raised the upcoming U.S. presidential election and repeated something one of the candidates had said that had blown me away for how horrible it was. One of my employees laughed and said how he liked how amusing and entertaining the candidate was and planned to pledge his vote. I snapped at him for choosing whom to back for president based on amusement. Whether my view was right or wrong was totally irrelevant. My action was totally wrong. I reflected on what I had done, and felt horrible for what amounted to just plain being mean. The employee is a great person and didn't deserve that. I apologized to him the next day when we next spoke. I also apologized to everyone else who had been at the dinner. And that was that. I obviously don't feel good about what I had done, but I also am not dwelling on it or letting it impact my interactions beyond the lesson I learned about not raising such issues or snapping at people the way I did.

If I were holding on to it, I might be biased in how I interact with that employee or others who had been there. I might be too soft on him due to guilt or fear that he'd branded me as a jerk, and so would need to overcompensate to undo that perception of me. Or maybe I'd continue to judge him for his view and treat him differently for that reason. Whether it's just about me feeling bad and carrying that pain or some non-ideal interaction with the employee or others, I'd be paying a price and our work product (and by extension, our company) would likely suffer.

I was able to contain my feelings and response to that Day because of my understanding of how dragging out the disappointment in myself can cost more than the thing I'm disappointed in myself for in the first place. I reflected on the situation as it happened and actively chose to address it head on and then move forward. The incident happened, and I can't change that. I can be responsible for it, and I can do better in the future. That is enough, so now it's about moving ahead so I can Do better each Day.

Ironically, the job I have at the time I'm writing this book is in the exact space as the model I built when I was a consultant. I don't just work in the space, but I actually run the whole operation. And the work I did back then played a direct part in me getting the job — even the mistake and what I learned from it. The reason I can be successful is that I've practiced Do a Day in the face of work challenges since that original, seemingly catastrophic mistake in order to become a better employee, coworker and leader. I'm more balanced today and can handle the ups and downs more fluidly as I move to the next challenge, knowing I can tackle it through Do a Day.

Work happens a Day at a time, though in today's world, so many jobs feel 24/7. But we still have the ability to segregate the hard work we have to do in a given moment, the mistakes we make or the problems we run into and keep them within their temporal and contextual boundaries. We can allow ourselves to enjoy things and be successful again despite all the tough stuff. We can get through the tough things on that Day they happen, and tomorrow, we Do a Day unencumbered by yesterday's trials and tribulations. We're more likely to succeed when we don't act under the weight of past missteps. Success begets success, and failure can stop it.

Inevitably, we will have bad Days. Things will go wrong or end up in a way we wish they didn't. And that's okay. The question is how you move past those moments to get back to success. To get back up and Do a Day again. Let's see how you can Do that after you have a bad Day.

THE END OF THE DAY

Let's recap the key messages from *Day 8. Do a Day at the Office* to see how Do a Day can help you through the tough moments in your work — whatever they may be:

- Do a Day applies directly to work challenges by helping contain them within their boundaries rather than letting them spiral into bigger problems

- The Do a Day approach at work is really about being more resilient and able to succeed in your next challenge despite any tough times you've faced before

- While it can take practice to Do a Day in the face of major work failures or problems, you can actively apply Do a Day in each situation you face so that it becomes more natural

DAY 9.
HAVING A BAD DAY

So far, I've shared specific situations or types of challenges from my experience that Do a Day directly applies to and shown how to use it in your own life in similar situations. I want to focus on something that can happen along the way as things don't always go perfectly or smoothly. No matter how great your goal, how strong your motivation is or how well you're succeeding, invariably you may come across tough days and setbacks or have times you feel derailed. In this chapter, I want to talk about those times and how to respond in those moments. It's ultimately about how you respond in these moments and what you do to recover when you stumble on your path as you Do a Day.

Success is fantastic and can be self-reinforcing. The better you do, the better you feel. And the better you feel, the more likely you are to keep at it because you feel invigorated and positive. But even the most positive, motivated, successful people can have off days. We can fail sometimes, get sick or injured or just be in a situation where we can't or don't make the choices we wished we could. Call it a bad day, going through a rough patch, being in a funk; whatever it is doesn't matter. The key is how you respond and recover. Ultimately, this is about staying on the path when things get tough.

This is where the Do a Day approach shines and shows that it's not just an achievement strategy, it's also a way to sustain.

The motivation I took from wanting a better life for myself and wanting to be a better father for my son drove me to want to be healthy. Taking a Do a Day approach to it got me to that place of health and wellness I knew I needed to be in. But what keeps me here, and what will continue to keep me here through the ups, downs, challenges and distractions of life? It is the same as what got me here — I Do a Day no matter what.

When I coach people on finding a true motivation, a key aspect is that it endures rather than being fleeting or temporal (see more about this in the chapter in section II called *Finding Your True Motivation to Do a Day*). Times change, desires change and interests wane. You need a motivation that will always be there regardless. For people who tell me their motivation is to look better or to feel better, I challenge them to dig deeper. Why? It's simple; if that's their motivation, and if it were enough to motivate them, then we wouldn't be having a conversation about how they're not living the way they want to.

Once you have your real motivation, it's as straightforward as saying, "I will Do a Day. Every day." Just like the idea of losing 100 pounds (or 15 or 400) can be too much to take all at once, the idea of working out and eating well *for the rest of your life* can feel like too much for many people. So we take each Day individually.

This helps you differentiate giving up in totality from giving up on a single Day. Think of learning to walk. Everyone learning to walk stumbles and falls. Everyone. And everyone who succeeds gets up at some point and tries again. No stumble or fall defines their ability to walk forever. They just get up and do it again. And again. And again. Going after any goal is the same — we will likely stumble, we will likely fall. When we Do a Day, we contain each fall in its own box so it doesn't stop us from walking.

Looking at the goal of living healthfully that so many of us have helps bring this into perspective and make it directly applicable. But this mentality holds for any of the tough times we face in the path of achieving and sustaining any goal, whether it be around our health, career, family, finances, friends, sports, etc.

When taking a Do a Day approach to eating healthfully, we make choices about what to eat *right here, right now*, without thinking about whether we'll make the best choices tomorrow, or regretting choices made yesterday. We don't punish ourselves with starvation because we overate last night at an event. Nor do we view making a poor choice one day as so disastrous to the big picture that we fall off the wagon and binge eat. No dietary stumble has the right to keep us from learning how to live a life of good nutrition.

You know the situation — you are on a diet and find yourself out with friends, at a work event or at a family function. You try to be "good," but end up having that thing you think you shouldn't, whether it's a piece (or two) of birthday cake, a plate of nachos, a slice of (or an entire) pizza or a beer (or six). You go home feeling defeated for how "bad" you were, and then you feel like you've thrown everything away. Your weakness and failure to be "good" have destroyed any progress you've *ever* made, and closed the door on success *from here forward*. How could you do this? How could you be so weak? You get depressed, upset with yourself, and fill your mind with negative talk about your failure or worse, your ability to succeed at all. So you eat more "bad" stuff because it's too late now, so you might as well enjoy yourself, right? But when you link dominos like this, you throw away opportunity and needlessly bring in emotional hurt.

Let's break it down to facts to understand this better. We're going to do a little math. If that's not your thing, don't worry — I'll take you through it. Let's say you've lost 15 pounds on your quest to live healthier. Now, at that birthday party last night, you had a piece of cake or a second piece of cake. How bad is it really? Well, that piece of cake is maybe 350 calories.[9] If it's really big and decadent or if you ate its twin sister when you went for seconds, perhaps it's a 700-calorie indulgence. Generally speaking, that's a tenth to a fifth of a pound, assuming it takes about 3,500 calories to lose a pound of body weight (this rule of thumb is a gross

---

[9] CalorieCount.com lists an average piece at 395, but I've simplified the numbers a little for this example.

over-simplification of how metabolism works, but my point holds, so hang with me a little longer). That means, in the grand scheme of the progress you've made, it's 0.67 percent. That is to say, it's a rounding error.

If you drink a 12-ounce glass of water before weighing yourself, you'll do more damage to your weight[10] than eating that piece of cake did. Instead of containing that choice in the current Day, by linking it to all Days past and future, you crumble over less than a 1 percent deviation. A rounding error. An irrelevant impact on your progress.

That's not to say this was a good choice for your physical health, but it may have been a good choice for your *emotional* health. Making that emotional health choice was smart, yet you negate that value by seeing it as a big failure physically. You end up robbing yourself of the emotional health benefit you were going for by overriding it with the physical judgment. And that doesn't even take into consideration the physical damage you'd do by using this "failure" from a small, poor choice as the catalyst to binge on junk food or give up on your quest of healthier eating overall.

In this way, Do a Day helps you reach your goal and maintain your success because it guides you down the path, while ensuring you don't stop walking simply because you faltered slightly for a moment. Or if you've stepped off the path you've set yourself on, you don't have to continue off the path — you can step right back into it and still get to where you're heading. There's still a path in front of you, you still know how to walk, and you can take each step, each Day, one at a time without the burden of past stumbles or the worry of how many steps lie ahead prompting you to quit.

The same goes for exercise. You go to the gym, go for a run or whatever activities you have and enjoy in your

---

[10] Of course, I don't mean that the water will do damage to your health, but rather that it will increase the number on the scale.

life, and just Do that activity on that Day. You don't over Do it today to make up for not Doing as much yesterday, or to bank extra in case you slack tomorrow. You don't beat yourself up because you missed today, and then stop going to the gym ever again (or perhaps until the next time you set a New Year's resolution to go to the gym). If you miss today, then you've simply missed today. Tomorrow, you get up and Do a Day.

Case in point, I set out almost by accident on a running streak that started on New Year's Eve in 2015. Next thing I knew, I had run at least 3.1 miles (5 kilometers) each day for about 10 days. When I realized what I had done, I decided I'd continue this streak. I didn't decide how long I'd do it for in total, but did decide to keep it up for the month of January at the very least. I'd worry about the rest of it when I got there.

January went well. I finished the month having run over 115 miles (about 20 more than 5K every day would have yielded), and I felt great (both physically and emotionally) about the accomplishment. I crossed into February, and thought I'd keep things going. I didn't care whether it was for the whole month or the rest of the year. Each Day I woke up, and chose to Do at least another 5K that Day. Until February 5th, when I was too sick to run.

I could have said, "Well, that's it, the streak is over, so I'll throw in the towel." And I could have said, "Oh no! I better run 10K tomorrow no matter how I feel because I have to make up for missing today!" I said and did neither of those things. Nor did I dwell on it or beat myself up at all for breaking the streak. Instead, I allowed my body the rest it needed. I paid attention to what it was telling me, and I nurtured it. The healthier choice was rest rather than running, and I was in this running thing because of my desire to be healthier, so the right answer was the clear one — rest.

And that approach, boxing my "bad" Day off from my prior streak of good Days and my potential for future good Days, allowed me the head space I needed to get back on my game when I woke up feeling better the next Day. And I Did it. And I've done it every Day since (it's been two weeks since I missed a Day as of this writing). Will I keep Doing it? That question doesn't weigh on my mind. If I can, I will. If I can't, I won't. But I won't let any *can* or *can't* define anything I've done or will do because I'm still on the journey and still healthy.

In my career, I've taken a lot of flights. A lot of long flights. A lot of long, all-day or all-night flights. Those flights have often impacted my workouts, either because I had to wake up so early to make my flight that I didn't have time to do my daily cardio, or because I was so exhausted after the flight that I just needed to get to bed. It's amazing how sitting there doing nothing physical for hours wipes me out.

What I learned long ago is trying to do a double workout the day before or after one of these flights ends up impacting a week or two of workout performance because it just adds to my exhaustion, and makes my recovery from travel take that much longer. Tying that day I've taken off to my overall physical performance was costing me about 13 other days of feeling good. How does that math add up? It doesn't, that's how.

Along the same line, when training for my first marathon, I got injured during a 10K trail race I did a month into my training. I was so focused on all the other days in my training plan, and how many workouts I needed to complete, that I pushed myself back out on the road much sooner than I should have. Pretty much my entire right side was not moving correctly (my hip was badly bruised, my quad was deeply injured and my knee was banged up). As a result, in the middle of a run I ended up very severely injuring my left calf, because of how I was compensating in my gait. It was so bad that I was stopped dead in my tracks, couldn't walk for several minutes, and then could barely hobble. And then a massive thunderstorm started (you have to love New England thunderstorms in summer). And I didn't have my phone with me. And I was a mile and a half from home. And

I had a meeting to get to in an hour. Thank goodness my wife decided to go drive around and look for me because I was gone for a while and the storm was so bad.

As bad as that day was, my decision to keep training because I was focused on the totality rather than an individual day ended up costing me a week of inactivity and pain, emotional distress, depression around potentially having to bag my marathon goal and a couple of weeks of scaled-back performance as I continued to rehab my calf. Not following a Do a Day approach after my race injury ended up costing me three to four times what I was afraid of losing in the first place, saying nothing of my mental state after my calf injury, when I had to work very hard to keep from constantly thinking my marathon goal was ruined. That certainly took more mental energy to keep in check than enduring a few days of rest after falling in that race would have taken.

When talking about how to look at bad days, I do want to point out what Do a Day isn't. It isn't an excuse to screw up. It isn't a way to consciously do what you shouldn't because you stop caring and can just close the lid on today's box and start again tomorrow. It's positivity and empowerment, not an excuse.

I believe that success begets success. I also believe that a mentality that accepts failure and laxity begets more failure and laxity toward achieving your goals. When you let yourself go one day (not just having a piece of cake, but feeling like today doesn't matter so you can go do anything with no consequences), you will create a mindset that allows for not caring. And not caring leads to not doing.

This chapter's message isn't about giving you a free pass to ignore the right path, or a way to cheat the system. Instead, it is about a way to view tough days when things don't go as planned.

After all, the "system" you would be cheating is yourself.

Remembering that the steps you took to get *here* will keep getting you *there* is how you Do it. Keep your motivations close, and remember to mindfully keep each choice — each Day — separate from all others. Today is today. Once you've made it to your goal, you stay successful through the same mindset and go for the next one. You Do a Day. Every Day.

THE END OF THE DAY

Day 9. Having a Bad Day focuses on the cost of choosing to not Do a Day or using a problem or slip-up as an excuse to stop.

- Success leads to more success, but failure only leads to more failure when you let it, so don't rob yourself of the chance to succeed again when times get tough

- The key is how you respond and recover

- Box your "bad" Day off from your "good" Days to get back on your game for the next Day

II. THE "WHY" & "WHAT" TO DO: MOTIVATION & GOALS

I hope sharing my experience and giving perspective on the various ways the Do a Day approach can get you to success has shown you what the philosophy is really about. To apply it, you need to start with two key things — you need to know what you're going for, and you need to know why you're going for it in the first place. Only you need to find them in the other order — motivation, then goals.

In this section, you're going to learn how to identify your "why": the reason you do things. Once you find your deep motivating reason, you can use it to achieve your "what": the things you want to do in your life. The order may seem backward to some people, but the reason for it is simple — if your "why" is a true motivation, it is the basis for your "what." If you have a goal and then search for the motivation to achieve it, the motivation won't be strong enough to keep you going.

Let's find your motivation, your "why," and then use the power of that "why" to define real goals that will transform your life for the better.

DAY 10.
FINDING YOUR TRUE MOTIVATION TO DO A DAY

In this first chapter of the second part of the book, I want to focus on motivation. You will learn to find what really motivates you deeply enough to transform your life. I will share what I've learned to be critical aspects of real motivation, and guide you on the discovery of what your true motivation is. You'll leave this chapter with the first fundamental building block you need to move ahead for the rest of your life.

The hardest part of Do a Day for almost everyone is finding the reason to do it. That reason is your *true* motivation. It's the real first step you must take, and the one almost everyone skips or doesn't even think of taking. It's also the main reason why people fail to reach their goals, so it's where I start the process with everyone I coach — it's the first Day you will Do.

So why is it first? Why don't you define a goal and then find the reason why you will do it? Well, doing things in that order often leads to your motivation falling short of what it takes to be a truly motivating factor. The motivation will be a byproduct of the goal rather than the underlying driver for reaching the goal. You need to first look within yourself to know the "why" in your life. Everything else follows from that.

The problem is that many people are too out of touch with themselves to know what drives them. Creating the right kind of motivation to ensure you are successful means *really* knowing yourself: your fears, your aspirations, your insecurities, your hopes, your dreams, your interests, your disinterests.

For me, I was big into introspection and self-development, but still hadn't found my real motivation until it hit me when my wife got sick (as I discussed in *From "The Fat Kid" to "A Fit Man"*). For others, it may simply be a function of time — not that you don't have it (as many of us claim), but that you aren't *making* it. We've heard it many times before from others or ourselves: "Oh, I would do that, but I just don't have the time to do it." Or, "I can't do that. I have to pick up the kids and take them to soccer practice, and then I have to make dinner, and then ABC, and then XYZ. Maybe if I had unlimited time, but I just don't have that kind of luxury."

The truth is, we all have the time — we just have to find it or make it.

People hear that and often push back about there only being 24 hours in a day, and there's no room left for any more to do. Yes, there's an ultimate maximum number of hours, but we're talking about how you use those hours smartly, and for now, I'm just talking about taking some of it to get to know yourself better. You can multitask and do some introspective thinking while you commute, shower, cook, clean, etc. You can do it while you work out, if you have the time to work out. Or you can create that time (e.g. run/bike/walk to work, walk or run during your lunch break) and then use it to think. Or you can give up or deprioritize something of lesser value. You have to make those judgment calls and the time will suddenly make itself. I know firsthand as someone who gave all the same reasons why I couldn't do something due to my time being too short. And then I found pockets of time I was wasting by dawdling or not multitasking when I could.

So what do I mean by the "right" motivation?

How do you know when you've found the real thing that will drive you to Do a Day and transform your life?

The key is to create or formalize a motivation that has four major attributes. It needs to be something that is:

1. Deep within you.
2. Enduring.
3. Profound.
4. Non-Material.

Deep Within You

Your true motivation must live in a very deep part of you. For the religious out there, I would say this is somewhere in your soul. It's something that is always with you, and so personal and strong, it could bring you to tears. For most parents, the answer is often tied to your kids. For some people I've worked with, it's something tied to their mortality. For others, it's about wanting a better life than what they grew up with. Wanting to feel pride in themselves every day, rather than shame or sadness, drives other people I've coached.

The thing is, I can't tell you what it is for you or give you a meaningful set of examples for you specifically because of the very nature of this component of real motivation. Only you can know what it will take, and a list here won't help unless I just happen to hit on your thing *and* you're even aware of what it might be. In that case, you don't need me to list it since you already know what it is. But most people don't know, and need help figuring it out. They need help knowing which questions to ask themselves to come to an understanding of themselves. This is where I spend the most time with clients when working on motivation — helping them see what's driving them.

The most common motivation I hear from people who are trying to exercise more and eat healthier is that they want "to feel better." They know they feel better when they work out and don't eat poorly, so they feel this is their deep motivation. Unfortunately, it isn't a good enough motivation, and I can prove it quite simply. Let me illustrate why by sharing the conversation that I have each time I hear this motivation. The people are different, but the words are pretty much always the same, and it goes like this:

Client:	"What's my motivation? Well, I feel better when I work out and don't eat junk, so that's my motivation. I want to feel better."
Me:	"I don't think it is. Tell me why you believe it is your real motivation?"
Client:	"Yeah, it is. I feel better when I work out regularly, and I *want* to feel better, so that's my motivation."
Me:	"It isn't. Let me ask you a question, and I think you'll see why it isn't. If it were, we wouldn't be talking about how you're not doing these healthier things. That is, *it's not actually motivating* you. How can it be your motivation if it isn't motivating you?"

Now some people get what I mean. They wouldn't be trying to convince me that this is their motivation, because they'd see that it is having no real impact on their behavior or drive once I point it out to them. The mere fact that they have to try to justify and explain it to me (or really to themselves) is proof that it isn't enough to be their real motivation.

The last person like this whom I was talking to was an "I'm always right" kind of guy, so he just looked angry with me for questioning him (that's OK — that's my job as a coach. I get to say the tough stuff you don't want to hear but secretly know inside). However, when I saw him the next day, he said he got it and I was totally right. It wasn't just about feeling better physically, but feeling *better about himself.* A subtle difference in words, but a very profound difference in meaning. It might be that he wants to feel better physically, but that's not enough to get him to change his behavior. Eating ice cream or drinking beer can make you feel better in the moment. Lounging around can make you feel better. You have no reason to choose exercise or healthy eating if the outcome from ice cream, beer and the couch are the same and take less effort. But when you choose those things all the time, you don't usually end up feeling better or *better about yourself.*

That's my point in pushing back on "to feel better" being a good enough motivation. Motivation must *motivate* you. It must change your choices and behavior. It's not just something you know — that's not good enough.

And as I discussed in the chapter *From "The Fat Kid" to "A Fit Man"* "deep within you" means the motivation has to be something inside of you, not something from the outside world. My original motivation to lose weight as a teenager was tied to how people saw me, whether I knew them or not. My drive depended on being judged by others. Not surprisingly, I ended up off course because that motivation couldn't last. When I found my *true* motivation in my deep love and devotion for my son and wanting to be the best father I can be to him, I found a motivation that not only has ensured I stay on the right path, but has actually driven me more and more as time goes on, rather than fading away. He might be "outside" of me literally, but being his father is within me, and I can assure you that boy is every bit as much in my heart and soul as I am.

What you need to ask yourself is this — what is so important to your very being that you can't imagine losing it or not having it in the first place?

That's the first and most important question in finding your true motivation. Let me explain what I believe are the key characteristics of true motivation, and then I will share some questions you can ask yourself to explore what that might be for you specifically.

Enduring

True motivation must endure. It shouldn't be something tied to a specific event that will pass. When I share my motivation, which is to be there and be a great example of health for my son throughout his life, it helps drive the point home. This isn't about a specific event I want to be fit for, like a high school reunion, wedding, life insurance exam I want a good rate for, bathing suit season or a marathon. My son isn't going anywhere, and my responsibilities to him as his father don't end.

Some people talk about wanting to ensure they have functional fitness in their retirement years so they can enjoy the fruits of their hard labor from when they worked. Whether it's travel, caring for grandchildren or just getting outside and enjoying the world around them, I know a lot of people who say this is why they stay fit.

My good friend and mentor, Dai Manuel, shared this idea with me when I interviewed him for my podcast years ago (you can watch the interview on YouTube at www.newbodi.es/daimanuel). He has a few motivators (like his kids and being healthy so he can be there for them and his wife), but a key one is so he and his wife can enjoy their free years later in life together, with neither of them sidelined for health reasons they could have avoided had they just made better choices earlier in life.

For others with some threat to their life in their world (e.g., chronic illness), they want to stay healthy because it keeps their illness at bay, which means they aren't suffering or aren't suffering as much as if they didn't work at their health. And their illness isn't going away, so this isn't about just getting through to some point of being cured, but rather about keeping stasis in their life at a level that allows them to participate in their life.

You can see that these aren't just enduring motivators, but they're also deeply personal. These components go hand-in-hand, and are often impossible to separate when you find what drives you.

Profound

If it isn't obvious yet, your motivators need to be big, powerful things in your life. They shouldn't be frivolous or petty. Surviving, inspiring your kids, being there to provide for your family, being there to enjoy life with your family — these are big, powerful, *profound* things.

For example, a motivation to look amazing so people are attracted to you, so you can get dates with attractive people, isn't profound. If that's what you think is your motivator, would that truly impact every decision point you face around your health? Can you see yourself making the right decision when faced with wanting to have some "bad" food, starting up smoking again or skipping a workout because an attractive person wouldn't go out with you if you did it? Obviously, you can skip a workout or have an ice cream occasionally. The point, however, is that the motivator should be present in every decision you make, and I find it hard to believe that a motivation that isn't profound would do that.

Even a motivation as superficial as the one we were just discussing can be reframed to serve a bigger purpose. Perhaps instead of just dating, the motivation is that you want to attain fitness to help you find "the one" so you can marry a person you're truly attracted to personally, emotionally and physically. That reason is much more profound, long lasting and holistic, and that means it's more likely to impact your choices than some fleeting, amorphous idea of looking good to get to go out on a date with random, attractive people.

Non-Material

Some people are motivated by money and having things. I'm not against money or things, but I *am* against those being your true motivators. I've certainly worked hard and been driven to succeed professionally, and by extension financially. I like nice things and being financially secure while providing a good life for my family.

But the problem with material motivators is that they're outside of you and can come and go. They might be big or expensive, but that doesn't make them profound. Indeed, they lack that deep connection to your inner self, and instead focus you on the outside world to things that are fleeting and not profound.

That's not to say that aspiring to be the CEO of a company is necessarily material. Materiality depends on the why — your reason. Do you want to do it because CEOs tend to be well paid, or do you want to do it because you want to be a leader with great responsibility and the ability to grab opportunity and transform an organization? If it's the latter, you will choose to invest in yourself for your personal and professional growth. You will work on inspiring others as a leader. You will work on developing your business savvy and acumen to find and seize opportunities, creating rewards and jobs for others. You may find that good health allows you to be more successful in this pursuit, as you feel better and have the energy to pursue your dreams as well as the mental clarity you need to win. While I'm speaking from my personal experience, there is also a lot of research on the positive impact of wellness and fitness on performance at work.

Bryce Hoffman, in his fantastic book *American Icon*, chronicles the story of Alan Mulally becoming the CEO of Ford to save the company and turn it into a highly successful business again.[11] Mulally had been one of the top executives at Boeing, and was already well paid. Ford and its peers were teetering on bankruptcy, so a job there carried a massive risk of being out of work with a tarnished record in short order. Mulally took the challenge because the chance to reshape and save a true American — if not global — icon was too motivating. Of course, he could do very well financially if he succeeded (and did), but the odds were against him and he didn't need the money. His motivation wasn't pay or title. His motivation was challenge and impact.

If it's about the pay alone, then you can make bad choices to get there — dealing drugs or being a paid assassin are probably more lucrative paths than working to be a CEO. If those sound absurd, what about looking at less

---

[11] Hoffman, Bryce, *American Icon*, Crown Publishing Group, New York, NY. ©2012.

blatantly criminal examples like Enron, WorldCom or Bernie Madoff's securities firm? Sure, even these business examples are extreme and a bit absurd, but you see what I mean? The material motivation doesn't drive a path of good, empowering choices.

What happens when you earn that dollar amount you were motivated to earn? Do you quit? Do you stop trying? What's keeping you going now?

Material things come and go. They don't endure. They're not profound. And they're certainly not deep within you.

A lot of books try to tell you what your motivation is or explicitly how to define it in workbook-like fashion. Because of the nature of what I think real motivation is, I don't believe it can come from such a process. I think the only path to the real motivation is to have that look inside of yourself at the deepest level, understand who you are and build your motivation from there.

While I can't tell you what *your* motivation is, I can leave you with some crucial questions you need to ask yourself once you've set the time to look within and find your motivation. This will start that introspective process and help you find your motivation.

Here are some of the questions to start exploring within yourself:

1. What are your most important values that define your sense of right and wrong, good and bad?
2. What is so important to your very being that you can't imagine losing it or not having it in the first place?
3. No matter what happens, what will you always care about?
4. If someone were to look back on your life, how would you want him or her to think you lived it? What do you want him or her to think you lived it for?

Answering these questions may not immediately spell out your own true motivation, but they will help you understand yourself and what makes you tick so that you can pull your motivation from that deeper understanding. That's the tough part of the process, but the part that is most crucial to create a true, lasting drive to do better and be better. We take that drive, apply it to a goal and get at it with each Day we Do.

Once you know why you are Doing a Day, you need to know what you're trying to achieve in that Day. Let's go find out which goal you will work toward when you Do a Day.

THE END OF THE DAY

In *Day 10. Finding Your True Motivation to Do a Day*, you learned about finding your true motivation to change.

- True motivation will be:
    o Deep within you
    o Enduring
    o Profound
    o Non-Material

- To find your own true motivation, it helps to reflect on deep aspects of yourself, including:
    o Your most important values
    o What you can't imagine losing or not having
    o What you will always care about
    o What purpose your life should serve

DAY 11.
SETTING SUCCESSFUL GOALS FOR SUCCESSFUL LIVES

Now that you've put the work in to understand what truly motivates you to improve your life, you can take that motivation and guide it toward a purpose. Goals will structure the improvement you seek by defining challenges, identifying actions and helping you plot a course to doing better and being better. In this chapter, you'll learn about the importance of setting good goals, and what a good and bad goal look like so you can ensure you build your own goals in a way that sets you up for a series of successes that combine into your new, enhanced life.

Goal-setting is a crucial step that a lot of people don't work hard enough at, because they don't want to, don't know how to or don't know that it matters. So many of us — an estimated 40 percent to 45 percent — set health-related goals every New Year's as part of the almost laughable practice of making New Year's resolutions. And do you know how many succeed? Eight percent.[12]

Many people fail to meet their goals because they lack the kind of motivation I talked about in the prior chapter. Turning the arbitrary page of a calendar from one year to the next is just not a good enough motivation for anyone. But even when you have the right motivation, the wrong goal can be just as likely to lead to failure. Goals contribute to failure when they:

---

[12] StatisticBrain.com
(http://www.statisticbrain.com/new-years-resolution-statistics)

- Are too big.
- Are too vague.
- Lack substance.
- Are unenjoyable.

Too Big

Goals that are too big can be crushing, demotivating and even impossible, as I've mentioned earlier in this book (see *The First Step* and *Having a Bad Day*). The number one New Year's resolution is also the most common "too big" goal, and that's to lose weight.[13] Specifically to lose *a lot* of weight, such as 25, 50 or even 100 pounds or more. A goal like that is *so* massive, and feels *so* far away that it leaves you both scared by its size and detached by its distance at the same time. It simultaneously pushes you away and feels irrelevant. Instead, we need goals we can be just a bit in awe of but can also touch.

Too Vague

The next common mistake people make in goal-setting is that they have vague goals. People often set goals like, "get fit," "go to the gym" or "eat better." Those are all good things, but let me ask you, what does "get fit" mean and how will you know when you've "gotten fit"? Or how often do you need to "go to the gym," because if you go just once, you've gone to the gym, so is the goal complete? Eat better than *what*? How often? How *much* better? And how do you define "better"? As you can see, these goals are vague, which means you can't tell if you're making clear progress toward achieving them, or when you're done — or even if there is such a thing as being done at all.

---

[13] StatisticBrain.com
(http://www.statisticbrain.com/new-years-resolution-statistics)

Lack Substance

Even if goals aren't vague, they can lack substance. They may not seem frivolous at the time, but in retrospect we often recognize that they weren't important enough things to focus on. Often these are fleeting or petty things, such as losing enough weight to fit into that great dress to make your ex feel jealous when you see each other at your mutual friend's wedding. It may not be vague, but it certainly isn't substantial in the grand scheme of your life.

Are Unenjoyable

I don't mean the key component of the goal is something that you don't get enjoyment from. I mean it is something more negative than just being the absence of joy. This pitfall is often common to health-related goals (e.g., eating some vegetable every day that you don't enjoy, doing some physical activity you don't like or even experience pain during — running takes top honors here), but can also be for non-health goals (e.g., reading some book you don't like but feel like you should, etc.). First, it's masochistic to create a goal around something you really don't enjoy. Second, how do you expect yourself to stick with a goal that requires you to do something you can't stand? Why would you try to brute-force-suck-it-up-grin-and-bear-it your way to completion? Why wouldn't you choose to build your goal around something you enjoy or at least don't despise? Dislike running and feel lots of pain when you do it? OK, there are probably 20 other exercises you can name within the next two minutes that you could do instead, and I'll bet one of them brings a touch of joy (for example, common exercises I recommend for people who don't like running are dancing, jumping on a trampoline, riding a bike, lifting weights, using an elliptical or swimming).

Some people feel a need to conquer something they don't like, or to prove to themselves that they have the mental fortitude to get through something unenjoyable. That is admirable, but usually not long-term sustainable. That approach almost always leads to failure since it's very hard to keep doing that which we don't enjoy. And when you don't enjoy an activity, inactivity becomes an obvious and enjoyable alternative that many people end up choosing. Instead, start by finding an alternate activity you enjoy to remove the propensity to opt for inactivity.

If those are some of the reasons why improper goal setting can lead to failure, how do we set goals that reinforce the journey to success? A common goal structure, and one I like to use best, is known as SMART, as in, "Let's set SMART goals for ourselves!" It's an acronym, and the letters stand for the crucial characteristics of good goals:

- **S**pecific
- **M**easurable
- **A**ction-oriented
- **R**ealistic
- **T**ime-bound

Let's take each of these in turn, while keeping in mind we not only want to create SMART goals, but goals that also don't fall into the pitfalls we discussed above.

Specific

This is probably the easiest one to overlook or under-value, but it's hugely important. This is the counter to the vagueness pitfall. We don't just say, "get fit," but rather we define this better and more specifically into something like, "vigorously exercise daily and eat healthier foods at all three meals so my annual physical shows that my numbers are finally in the healthy range."

Measurable

That's a great start, but let's build on it with the next letter in the acronym — *Measurable*. It means you need to put some numbers around the goal so you can see if you're hitting it, surpassing it or have work left to do. You can track progress toward the goal along the way with each Day you Do. Don't just say, "lose weight," but rather say, "lose 15 pounds." Or if the goal is vigorous exercise, define the measurement of "vigorous" with something tied to heart rate. Or you could define the actual numbers you're going for in your annual physical like resting heart rate, cholesterol, body weight or blood pressure. These measurements make tracking your progress possible.

Action-Oriented

Next, we need goals that are action-oriented. This isn't strictly used for fitness goals, though you may think it is since it sounds like "action" must mean something like working out. The reason we need the goal to be action-oriented is because you have to *do something* to make it happen. A goal isn't just achieved by magic, so we need to structure it in a way that helps show us how we'll get there. In the goal about results at my physical, it's not just, "have all tests at my annual physical come back normal," or even the same thing with the specific, measurable test results in them like, "have cholesterol under 200 at my next annual physical." Rather it's about *doing something* to get the results to be in the normal range — work out and eat better. In the "lose weight" example, *you* have to lose it. It isn't just lost. Don't set a goal like, "have the scale say 180 instead of 195." After all, how do we Do a Day if there's nothing for us to Do in the first place? Sure, tomorrow will happen regardless of what we Do, but to truly *live* tomorrow, we have to Do something during that Day.

Realistic

Setting realistic, reasonable goals comes next, and it's important to get the balance right here. Goals need to push you and make you stretch yourself in the context in which you are starting. You need to be sure you don't go so far with the stretch that you've gone into the realm of genuine impossibility.

I often use a work example to illustrate the point. I used to manage a team that had at least doubled its revenue in each of the previous two years from $1 million to $4 million, and then to $8 million. Guess what goal senior leadership handed down to us for year three? Sixteen million dollars. But going from one to four or even four to eight is much easier than going from eight to 16 — in fact, going from eight to 16 is twice as hard as going from four to eight (adding $8 million instead of $4 million). And guess how that year went? We ended the year at $12 million, but our people felt demoralized despite growing by $4 million from $8 million to $12 million while the market fell apart during the financial crisis.

The team members should have been pushed to grow 50 percent to 65 percent, then felt energized that they were doing it because they were really doing a fantastic job and showing progress while several competitors were shrinking (and many were going out of business or being acquired).

You can imagine how weight loss is a common area in which people make similar mistakes — you want a true goal that will push you to take it seriously and work hard, while being careful not to set one you could rarely achieve regardless of effort.

For example, I've mentioned a few times now the rule of thumb that you can safely and consistently lose one to two pounds a week (after an initial faster burn the first week or two).[14] This depends on how much you weigh relative to where you should be,[15] but if we start with this one- to two-pound premise, then saying you could lose 65 pounds in a

---

[14] Initial weight loss often includes water weight, so it can be as high as five or six pounds (or more) for many people.

[15] You lose weight faster when you are bigger, as you burn more calories when you weigh more. That means your weight loss will vary versus other people, but also versus yourself as you progress toward your goal and may see a slowdown in your burn.

year would be a big yet achievable goal. When I was at my biggest, I had about 80-90 pounds to lose, so 65 would be tough yet doable and, importantly, hugely beneficial. I'd be well on my way to getting to a truly healthy weight.

Today, I really shouldn't lose any weight, but maybe I have two or three pounds to lose sometimes.[16] If I set a goal of 65 pounds, achieving it would likely kill me. It's an absurd goal. In the same way, setting a goal of losing two or three pounds back when I was obese would have been too easy and had no real impact on anything. I wouldn't even have needed to try all that much, or I'd try for the one week it would take to do it, and then let my foot off the gas and gain it right back (if not more). It's an irrelevant goal. Don't just set reasonable goals, but set *contextually* reasonable, stretch goals.

Time-Bound

Goals need to be time-bound. That's been the missing component to all of the example goals I gave — over what time period? Lose 65 pounds *this year*. Don't just "go to the gym more," but go to the gym at least four times *per week for at least the rest of the year*. Even my "annual physical" example doesn't say *which* annual physical I'm gunning for. Otherwise, you could give yourself a pass this year without breaking your goal and just shoot for next year's physical. And what if you said, "this year's physical," but haven't even scheduled it yet? You could then use that loophole to get out of it for a while, too.

I will make one caveat on the time component. Don't confuse that with a finish line after which you can just go back to your old ways. Instead, if you have a time by which you want to reach your goal, cross that finish line and set a new goal that's a second step after the first finish line. For example, when I was 80-90 pounds overweight, if I set a goal

---

[16] In reality, that means I don't really need to lose weight as this is a normal fluctuation from day to day or week to week.

to lose 65 pounds in a year, then I would set a goal the next year to lose the remaining 15-25 pounds and maintain my new weight going forward — a new SMART goal. It's about hitting your goal, and then living your life from this new, better place you've achieved.

*   *   *

This approach works perfectly when you decide to Do a Day and you're in the midst of that series of Days. Something I always tell people when setting a goal is to set little goals along the way. If your goal is to lose 65 pounds this year, then try to lose at least one pound a week. That gets you 52 pounds, so you need to push yourself to make up the last 13 along the way (that is, you need some two-pound weeks mixed in there). This act of breaking your goal down into weekly mini-goals provides a few key benefits.

First, the big goal may still be too big for everyday life. Do you know what to do each day to lose 65 pounds over 12 months? What are you striving for *today*? Break it down to the Day you are going to Do, and think about what you're trying to achieve within that day. If you were trying to save over $500 this year, then you can do it by saving $10 a week, or at least one to two dollars a day (or two a day during the week and none over the weekend). Whatever the bigger goal is, you can break it down into interim periods and sub-goals to make the actions and objectives for each Day clear and tangible.

Second, I'm a firm believer in the virtuous cycle of success. That is, success begets success. When you do well, you feel good, and you're more likely to do well again. When we create shorter-term goals that add up to our big goal, we create a path to win our way to overall achievement. And that is *very* rewarding and uplifting. I say this to everyone I've ever coached: "You will win your way to success."

This is a common tactic for runners who are tired during a run or a race. Here's how it works: Don't think about the total miles you have left right now, which can be daunting. Instead, pick a point in the distance like a road sign or building and run to that. And only that. Don't think about anything beyond that point. And once you get there, recognize that you achieved it and allow yourself to feel good about that because you got somewhere despite being tired. Then pick another point, run to it and celebrate inside.

I did this on a run while I was in New York for some meetings. My plan was to do at least eight miles through the city. If you haven't run in New York City, going out early in the morning for a run through Manhattan, Central Park or the path along the Hudson River is fantastic. I had been limited in how much time I had to run lately, and often couldn't run outside due to weather. The stars aligned on this trip with both time and weather on my side, so I wanted to be sure I made the most of it. I found myself getting tired well before the halfway mark that morning. And my GPS watch kept stopping because my mittens were bumping up against the stop/start button, so I was getting frustrated that I didn't know how far I had run, what my pacing was or for how long I had been going.

The sum total of the physical and mental challenges was that I was having a lot of trouble keeping myself going. I didn't have my phone, cash or a credit card with me, so I had no choice but to keep running. But, *man*, was it hard! I had a rough sense of my distance based on the rule of thumb that 20 North-South blocks are equal to a mile in New York City, so after turning around just below SoHo, I set a goal to get to 30th Street on my way to 50th. If I got to 30th, I'd be happy with my run and perseverance.

I was doing OK physically into the low 20s — not great, but good enough to keep going — so it was very doable, but still took pushing mentally. I was also trying to get to Lexington Avenue from 6th Avenue, so this wasn't just 10 blocks (or a half-mile) to 30th, but probably another quarter to half a mile to go across town a bit. But I just focused on each block, and watched the numbers grow every few strides. On 22nd, the goal was 23rd. No thoughts beyond

23rd, and none from before that. Just get to the street sign that read, "23rd ST."

I decided I needed to get to Lexington Avenue and have the weight of crossing town off my shoulders, since the blocks are longer going across town than going up or down. I got to Lexington Avenue at 26th — four blocks to go. "You've got this!" I literally said out loud. It was early in the morning, so no one was around to hear me or for me to feel embarrassed. With each block, I called out a little, "Woo!" I crossed 30th much sooner than I thought I would because the approach was lightening my legs and lifting me up. I found that I didn't care about my watch issues anymore, either. I was winning my way to the finish line one block at a time, and I was speeding up despite being tired and physically being more depleted with each stride. And, yes, my watch was tracking this part of my run, so I knew I was speeding up in reality and not just in my mind.

With 30th blowing by so fast, I immediately shouted, "Let's go for 40th!" And I did the same thing, only now there were some people around, so my shouting became a little more subdued. I'll admit 40th was tougher since that was 10 blocks rather than just the four from 26th, but I did it just fine, and was still speeding along. And you can guess what happened next — I went for 50th, right? Wrong. I went *past* 50th. OK, not that much, but I went to the end of the block at 51st, passing my hotel, and then walked back to the hotel to cool down. No, it's not a massive difference, but if I had continued on the feeling of desperation and exhaustion I felt starting earlier in my run when I was focused on getting all the way from downtown to my hotel in Midtown, I would have slogged it out and almost definitely stopped the moment I crossed safely to the other side of the block that my hotel was on. Or given myself a pass to stop short of 50th, and then walked to the hotel to cool down. And I certainly wouldn't have been speeding up toward the end. Instead, I broke the goal into smaller ones that would come much faster and won them all. I took those wins and used them as fuel to get to the end. Each block was like a Day. I chose to Do a Day one block at a time.

One thing I believe we must add to SMART goals is an E for *Enduring*. We aren't setting goals that we hit, only to fall back into our life the way it was. We're setting goals that transform our life into a way that endures. Remember, we are motivated by something enduring, so we need a path of goals that keeps up with our motivation. It must be something sustainable. That can be one single goal, or a series of goals that build on each other. Regardless of how you endure, you want to have a new life, not just a piece of it.

How do you set meaningful goals that position you for success while pushing you to achieve? Simple — you follow the steps outlined in this chapter. Start with your *true* motivation, and then understand what you need to complete to speak to that motivation and your future being as you want it. Take a stab at writing a SMART goal, checking that it doesn't fall into any of the pitfalls of being too big, vague, lacking substance or being something you don't enjoy, and then plot a path of smaller achievements that get you to the final goal.

THE END OF THE DAY

In *Day 11. Setting Successful Goals for Successful Lives*, you learned about setting the right goals to ensure you'll meet them.

- Poorly defined goals can set you up for failure, and often have the following traits:
    o Are too big
    o Are too vague
    o Lack substance
    o Are unenjoyable

- Well-built goals can set you up for success; using the acronym SMART can help you create great goals:
    o Specific
    o Measurable
    o Action-oriented
    o Realistic
    o Time-bound

- Win your way through your life of improvement through a series of goals that build off each other, with each success leading to the next

III. TAKE ACTION: HOW TO DO A DAY

Now that you've read a lot of ways that Do a Day has helped me live better and help others change their lives, the time has come in this section of the book to give some specific guidance that can help you figure out how to put this approach into action for yourself. It's not so much to spell out exactly what you *need* to do each day, but to give you some ideas about what you *could* do.

At this point, you should be inspired and enlightened as to what this approach is all about; you should be getting in touch with your true motivation and know what goal (or goals) you want to achieve. Now what you may need are some specific, helpful ideas to get the ball rolling. You could benefit from the seeds to start growing a series of Days of success.

Not everything I share will be an exact fit for your situation, so I invite you to find a way to evolve what I present into a sustainable plan for yourself. And remember, most crucially, the first two steps you need to do before starting any of these example approaches is to find your real motivation and build meaningful goals that set you up for success.

Lastly, I'd be an irresponsible certified personal trainer if I didn't say that I am not *your* certified personal trainer. I don't know your background, medical situation, life context, motivation or goals. What I share in the next few chapters isn't meant to be specific to you, and may in fact not work for you or speak to your situation at all. The best bet is to read it, be inspired and design something that works for your situation. If you're not sure how to do that, then I highly recommend finding a health and fitness professional[17] you click with to design the actions you will Do each Day.

Let's look at a few ways you can Do a Day for better fitness, for eating well and for your life as a whole.

---

[17] The best starting place is to get a referral from someone you trust. If that isn't an option or you don't find someone who would work well for you, you can search the IDEA Health & Fitness Association online directory at http://www.ideafit.com/fitnessconnect

DAY 12.
DO A DAY FOR BETTER FITNESS

People have many different starting points for their fitness, and different goals for where they want to take it. In this chapter, I share example approaches that are just that — examples. They can serve as starting points from which you can create something more specific to your needs. And if you don't think you know what to do, you can experiment to find what you like and works best for you, or consider finding a personal trainer to help you build a plan for your specific fitness level and goals. When you have a clear motivation and goal, a trainer can be much more helpful than if you show up at your first session bright-eyed, bushy-tailed and shrugging your shoulders.

Other than building a plan yourself, or hiring a trainer, there is a huge array of options out there to help you. YouTube has a lot of great fitness channels with free workout programs and routines. Some great channels to consider are BodyRock and GymRa. FitFluential (of which I'm an ambassador) regularly produces workout routines and ideas at fitfluential.com. There are Facebook fitness challenge groups you can join, like Dai Manuel's Whole Life Fitness Power 30 (30 minutes a day — just 2 percent of your day — for your betterment). Dai's approach is also outlined in his fantastic book, *The Whole Life Fitness Manifesto*, which you can get at many bookstores, Amazon (print and Kindle), iBooks, and more. Just visit wholelifefitnessmanifesto.com or search Amazon or the iTunes store. You can also purchase exercise-at-home programs like P90X from Beachbody. Basically, there are a lot of free and paid options that you can do wherever you are most comfortable and can fit into your life.

Now I'd like to take you through examples I've created for different levels of experience: newbies, weekend warriors and full-on exercisers.

The Newbie

You're new to exercise. You may be in less-than-ideal shape, with limited range of motion, muscle tone, coordination or knowledge of what to do to get fit. And you're not sure how to fit exercise into your life, but there are some major positives to talk about. You know *why* you are going to do it (your motivation), and why that motivation drives you. And you know what "it" is (your goal) so you have a direction that you can see clearly and markers to keep you on the right path along the way. Fantastic!

A great way to start is to use one of so many 30-day challenges out there. But we're going to do this a bit differently because 30 days does not a life make. The Internet is full of coaches, trainers and fitness challenge groups who put out challenges for a month. They have downloadable calendars that tell you what to do each day. The ones I like to use with people in this "new to exercise" group are things like push-up, wall-sit, lunge, squat, plank and crunch challenges. I do these quite often myself, having done burpee, wall-sit and plank challenges most recently.

You start with some number on day one, and each day you add an increment. For time-based ones like planks and wall-sits, typically you will start with 15 or 30 seconds, and add five seconds for each successive day. For ones based on repetitions, like push-ups, lunges and squats, you start with some number (this varies based more on skill than the time-based ones usually, so start with a doable number, but one that you have to work to finish — for you, maybe it's 10, or maybe it's two), and you add one more each day. If you start with five push-ups, by the end of the month, you're doing 35 or 36 — maybe more. And if five was tough, I bet you never thought you could do thirty-something, right? You did it by adding a little bit on top of what you achieved each successive day.

Get that? *Each successive day.* That is, you Do a Day. And like my marathon training example, each day builds you up a little bit more so you're always ready for the next day's incremental increase and the sum total of the days leaves you in a better place, ready to tackle whatever is next.

The twist is that you don't let the challenge end when the first month is done. Instead, the first month's challenge links to another challenge. If you want to step up the challenge and have a greater impact on yourself, do more than one challenge each month. Create little routines that build each day as you Do a Day. You can then start the next month's challenge from a higher starting point than the prior month, and keep building. Next thing you know, you've created an impactful workout routine made up of daily successes. How great will that feel physically and emotionally?

There are other ways to do this, too. You can do it with cardio, for example running for one minute on day one, and then adding 30 seconds each successive day. By the end of the month, you'll be covering about two miles, whereas you couldn't even run more than a minute or two when you started. Or you could do a run/walk program, where you start with a 15-minute mix made up of four minutes of walking followed by 30 seconds of running, done three times over, and finished up with a cool-down walk for the final minute and a half. Each day, you add five seconds to the run period, and take it away from each walk period. When you get to a minute of running, you can consider moving to a 1:1 ratio of one minute walking and one minute running. The next month, you add a little more time to the total. If you have a tough day and do more walking, or don't up the running time, that's OK. You still did the Day, and when tomorrow comes, you can go into it without judgment of yesterday. You've still built a foundation, kept on the path and are still achieving. You keep tough times in perspective on your path to overall success and you don't allow yourself to worry about how long your run periods will be a month from now.

You can do all of these things — do a few of the bodyweight exercise challenges and then a cardio challenge to create a 20- to 30-minute workout routine of mixed activity. Or you could get there over time by plotting out a series of monthly challenges. Start big enough to challenge yourself, but not so big that you quit. Sustainable yet challenging is the name of the game.

The key is to start with something that respects that you don't do any exercise today. Start small and manageable. Succeed and then build. As you start to rack up wins — Days you've Done — you will start to find the time to do more where you didn't think you possibly could work exercise into your life before. You'll *want* to keep racking up the wins. You'll want to keep feeling better.

Isn't this exciting? Writing this reminds me of my own transformation and how years of feeling like a failure were transformed through small successes that I focused on each day without feeling the weight of my past "failures" or of all I still had to do. I was free to just enjoy making a better life for myself. And you're going to be in that same place. Amazing!

The Weekend Warrior

Ah, the weekend warrior. You play pickup football with the guys. You go golfing. You ride bikes with the kids. Walk with your spouse or friend, or maybe even get out for a quick run Saturday morning while the kids watch cartoons or have soccer practice. You have *some* fitness, and you have a sense of the kinds of things you like doing, but you're not serious about it. You used to work out and were in shape in college, but life happened and you look like most Americans — you're not obese, but when people say you're healthy, they put the word in quotation marks. Or they say things like, "Oh, he's got a *healthy* neck," where "healthy" means big and solid like a tree trunk. The way I described myself was that I was in *a* shape rather than in shape.

The biggest part of the puzzle here is finding time. You already know what you would do with it, but you don't know where the time would come from. For this group, I'd suggest two things — wake up a few minutes earlier (start with five minutes — totally doable), or look hard at how you spend your day and very honestly critique whether you're wasting time somewhere (for example, getting lost in Facebook).[18] Here's a tip that helps almost everyone — stop taking your smartphone into the bathroom. Shocking suggestion, right? Same goes for reading material, paperwork or any other distraction. I'd bet you end up taking much less time in there. And that time can go to something for your body. Removing these black holes of time from your day may mean you can work out *and* sleep later. You'd be surprised.

Next, keep that warrior action on the weekend. You're Doing those Days already, so just keep at it. We're going to add the other Days to the mix. Using the time you just earned back through a slight reduction in time spent unproductively, find something active you can do. For some, that might be going to a gym, but it doesn't have to be. You can do things at home, whether inside or outside. If you have exercise equipment, that's great — use it. If not, that's great, too. Use your body and basic things around your house like stairs and chairs. You can dance, run around your block or go for a quick bike ride, or do the exercises I talked about above for the newbie. If you do them back-to-back without breaks, you will end up conditioning not only your muscles, but your heart, too.

Let me also take a moment to dispel the notion that you have to do an hour of cardio to get any benefit. I think

---

[18] You can reduce your temptation to use Facebook or other social media platforms on your mobile phone or tablet if you move the application icons off the main screen.

this idea is where a big part of the "I don't have the time" mentality comes from. My friend and mentor Dai Manuel's 30-minute Whole Life Fitness Power 30 program (that's about 2 percent of your day, or 3 percent of your waking day) only includes 15 minutes of cardio work. As a member of the challenge group he runs for people in the program, I've seen firsthand how transformative a purposeful 30-minute program with 15 minutes of actual, physical exercise can be. In the same way I'm asking you not to be unproductive when you're not working out, I'm suggesting you can be more productive while you *are* working out, and therefore don't need to devote huge portions of your day to it.

The Exerciser

You already work out. It's part of your life on a regular basis. But maybe you're not getting the results you want anymore, it's lost the excitement or isn't interesting to you anymore (if it ever was) or you feel like you need a bit of a reboot to get your mojo back. It's become more a matter of course, where you're just a robot going blindly through the motions. You get on a piece of cardio equipment, open a magazine or turn on the TV and tune out while the clock runs down. Did you work out hard? Did you get a benefit? Who knows, but you did read an interesting piece on the history of waffle irons. Or maybe it was about University of Oregon track coach Bill Bowerman, who co-founded Nike and ruined his wife's new waffle iron making shoe soles for his runners. Either way, you went to the gym and did your time, right?

The way most people exercise is like this — without purpose. That leads to losing interest in it. But you have purpose now — you know *why* and *what* you're working out for. Take that drive and use it to make your workouts more interesting and productive.

A workout missing purpose is typically one where you get on a machine at the gym, set the time and resistance and then tune out. You might be on the manual setting, or maybe you pick a program that varies the incline or resistance, but when it does, you're engrossed in something you're reading or a show you're watching, and don't alter your effort. That's what we're going to change when you Do a Day. We're going to be present in the moment and bring purpose, intent and focus back in. And you'll enjoy the workout as a result.

One key tool to try here is intervals. Specifically, High Intensity Interval Training or HIIT.[19] This is where you use short bursts of near-maximum effort to spike your heart rate, muscle involvement, breathing — everything. This stress creates two great benefits. First, the way we build muscle (including heart muscle) is to make micro-tears in the muscle fibers, which then heal stronger. Second, this approach of bursts of intensity leads to a higher metabolism for a longer time after the workout than a steady-state workout would have produced. Studies show that the "burn" from HIIT workouts can last up to 48 hours, whereas the burn from steady-state cardio workouts lasts only a few hours. That's right: When you work out, you don't just burn calories while you're working out. Your body continues to burn as it returns to its cooled-down resting state over time, and HIIT workouts just take longer to return to rest than constant-intensity workouts. You probably have seen this effect in action yourself if you've ever worked out and had to rush through taking a shower and getting dressed. You end up getting sweaty again after your shower because your body is still burning from the workout at a pretty high level.

Many cardio machines have interval programs in them that you can use, which is great. They force you to train using intervals without having to do the planning

---

[19] You may also hear the term Tabata, which is another kind of HIIT with a more specific pattern to it named after its creator, Dr. Izumi Tabata. It involves doing 20 seconds of ultra-intense effort followed by 10 seconds of rest, repeated continuously for four minutes (eight rounds).

yourself. For those that don't have these programs or if you're working out without a machine (e.g., biking, running, swimming), here's how you do it:

Warm-up: Start with a warm-up where you slowly increase the difficulty from easy to a moderate level over the course of three to five minutes, depending on the total length of the workout you're going to do.

Interval: Next, you enter the interval phase. Depending on the length of your workout, do 30 seconds of hard effort followed by a minute of recovery effort. For example, on my elliptical, I set the hard effort at a 16 out of 20 levels, and the recovery is done at a 10 out of 20 (the machine sets this based on my choosing 16). That's what feels right for me, but you need to know what is hard and easy for you. And 30-second intervals make sense if you're doing a 15-minute workout, but if you're doing something more like 30 minutes, go for one-minute intervals (still with one minute of recovery). The key with machines like this is not to let the interval come and go without increasing your effort. Many machines let you get away with this. Pay attention, and amp it up when the interval hits.

Cool-Down: Remember what you did for your warm-up? Now do the same thing in reverse (from moderate to easy) to cool down. This is probably the most overlooked part of an interval workout, or the one people ditch because it doesn't feel like work. You would do a slightly shorter cool-down than you did for your warm-up (two to three minutes, typically).

While that's a general approach to HIIT training based on my elliptical example, here are some ideas on settings and ways you can do HIIT training:

Treadmill Running: It can be harder to ignore the interval on a treadmill because the belt will speed up or the incline will increase (or both). If you don't have an automatic program, you can increase the speed by a full mile per hour or 30 seconds to one minute of pace (going from a nine-minute mile to an eight, for example) and you can even increase the incline by one to two degrees.

Running Outside: If you're running outside (or on an indoor track), sprint while you count to 20 (count on each inhalation or exhalation, but not both, to help control the speed with which you count). My marathon coach gave me what became my favorite workout that fits the bill well here. They're called strides, and you can do them at the end or middle of any run (or both). They are fun, make the run more interesting and help open your hips up so you feel better after the run. I remember dreading them before doing them the first time, but I ended up only minding the part of the run *before* I did them as it was a little boring.

My workout started with running four miles at a steady pace, then doing four sets of strides (or "stride repeats" for runners). They involved ramping up to 90 percent of my max effort and back down to my recovery effort over the course of a tenth of a mile (picture a hill where you speed up in the first .05 mile, and then slow down in the back 0.05 mile), and then running at recovery pace for a quarter mile. I can honestly say there were runs where I was just not feeling it during the four miles, and thought about quitting (not my style to quit, but I thought about it at least).

Once I got into the strides, my view of the run would change, and I'd get back home and my only memory of the run was a super positive one. It wasn't until I ran a stride workout with a friend that I realized that my short-term memory was being rewritten by the strides, since he brought up how I was making him want to quit in the first part of the run!

Fartleks: Yes, you read that right. It's a Swedish word that means "speed play." It's a different kind of interval where it's not about intensity, but style or form. That is, you run normally for a minute, then run sideways for a minute with one leg leading, then sideways for a minute with the other leg leading, then run backward for a minute, then run forward but with skips or mini-jumps for a minute, then run by lunging for a minute, then run carioca[20] for a minute, then back to normal. What you do doesn't matter so long as you do a variety of things. Then once you've completed a full set of these various moves, you do the pattern over again. You can do this running outside, indoors, on a treadmill — anywhere.

You can do it swimming (change strokes on each lap) or walking. Believe it or not, you can also do it biking — if you're on a road bike, go to the drops, hoods, sit up holding the straight part of the handlebar; come out of the saddle and pedal standing up; pedal one-legged (if you're clipped in); drop a gear and change your cadence, spin backward when you're going downhill or have enough momentum on a flat surface, etc. The variety makes things fun and interesting while also working different muscles or the same muscles differently.

What you'll find is that you have more fun on these workouts because you're more present in them and get the

---

[20] Not Karaoke. Carioca is a sideways move where one leg crosses over in front of and behind the other one. It's used in many running drills in practice for football or football teams (all types: soccer, American football, Australian rules football, etc.), boot camps, etc. Search for a video of it on YouTube as I've yet to see a way to describe it that leads the reader to know how to do it.

whole "variety is the spice of life" benefit. You aren't just shutting your mind off and going through the motions, which can feel like you're just waiting for the clock to run out. Who has mojo doing that? No one. When you do intervals of any kind, you force yourself to pay attention and be interested in the workout, which makes it more enjoyable.

Aside from enjoying the workout more, the additional benefit of HIIT workouts is that you can do *less* of a workout to get the same (or better) result, so you end up with more time in your day. You don't need to plop yourself on a bike for an hour and be miserable when you can do a 25-minute HIIT workout on that bike and really push your fitness to the next level. You end up saving more than half the time and not because you quit early, but because you worked out smarter and more efficiently. Give it a try, and I bet you'll see immediately via the amount you sweat and how tired you are physically (vs. mentally, which is usually what an hour on a cardio machine will do if your brain is tuned out the whole time).

So how does an HIIT approach fit with Do a Day? Simple — you won't keep Doing Days if you aren't enjoying them. And you aren't really Doing a Day if you are going through it mindlessly. Intervals not only give you better results but they make you present in your quest for fitness, which is an uplifting, energizing way to go about it. You come out of the workout not feeling like you *had* to do it, but that you just achieved something. And remember, success begets success. You will wake up the next day, ready to Do a Day again because you enjoy it.

THE END OF THE DAY

Day 12. Do a Day for Better Fitness shared some ideas for implementing Do a Day for better fitness:

- No matter where you're starting from, there are ways to create time in your day, and resources that cost nothing to start being more active

- Newbies can use 30-day challenge programs to start to build fitness from scratch

- Weekend Warriors can expand their current activity levels across more days by mindfully reducing unproductive time, and mindfully increasing the impact of the time they spend working out

- Existing exercisers can rekindle their interest in being active through trying new things, or using a more productive approach like HIIT to spice things up and drive results

DAY 13.
DO A DAY TO EAT WELL

Let me start this chapter by defining the word "diet" because I think it has been boxed into a corner in Western society. We think of diet as something you do — it's either a verb (e.g., I'm dieting this month because I have my high school reunion coming up) or a short-term noun (e.g., I'm doing this new diet where you eat nothing but pickles for nine days).[21] Diet is neither of those things (though those are acceptable uses of the word). It's not a shake for breakfast, a shake for lunch and a sensible dinner. When *I* talk about diet, I talk about it with a capital D. It is *what we eat, every day, for our lives*. This is the meaning of the word we must focus on to create a sustainable and enduring healthy life.

Diet is not black and white; rather, it's a continuum. One smart choice is better than none, and more smart choices are better than fewer. If you won't[22] go 100 percent on a better path, that isn't a reason to quit completely or not even start. I have worked with people to look at what they eat, and I get a lot of, "Well, I can't give up milk in my coffee, so I don't see the point to even try to cut out dairy." They throw away the ability to move further along the continuum because of one small item.

This dairy example is more than an illustration, as there are a few benefits here. Many people have issues

---

[21] I don't think there's a diet like this, but I think you get what I mean … and are also equally afraid that there may well be a diet like this at some point. I don't want to call out any specific diets here because I don't want to get an angry letter from any diet creator's lawyers, and my point applies across *all* short-term or fad diets.

[22] I think most people *can*, but have an aversion to doing so, or latch on to certain things and decide they *won't*.

digesting dairy (whether they know it or not). And many people also eat far too much sugar. In addition to being hard to digest for many people, dairy is very high in sugar. Taking out as much dairy as possible is better than just throwing your hands up and saying, "Oh well." Can't live without a splash of it in your coffee? That's okay. Try removing it elsewhere. Or better yet, try coconut or almond milk. They tend to taste better than soy milk and also go very well with coffee.

Think that dairy has crucial health benefits that make it required in a healthy Diet, like vitamin D and calcium? It does, but they're not as crucial or helping you as much as you think. The vitamin D in milk doesn't get absorbed or activated in our bodies that well. Sunlight exposure does more for you. While you can get calcium from other foods, there are several recent studies that conclude calcium supplementation doesn't help with bone strength, so perhaps the logic of requiring it at all isn't as sound as we once thought.[23] Lastly, don't forget that huge portions of the world's population have lived without dairy, including some of the longest-lived, healthiest populations, such as the Japanese. And vegans go without dairy, and somehow we aren't all dying young or breaking all of our bones due to them being brittle. My point isn't to bash dairy, but to point out that it isn't as crucial as some might argue, and there are clear benefits to removing it while you can easily get the benefits of dairy from other sources.

While removing dairy is a great way to cut back on sugar, the idea goes well beyond dairy — you can apply the same logic to the bigger picture. Another person I worked with had done a cleanse diet (lowercase D) and now was trying to eat healthily going forward. In the cleanse phase, she had cut a lot of foods out of her diet, including dairy and

---

[23] Whiteman, Honor, "Increasing Calcium Intake 'Does Not Improve Bone Health of Seniors,'" Medical News Today, September 30, 2015, http://www.medicalnewstoday.com/articles/300219.php

non-fiber carbs like bread and pasta. Post-cleanse, she felt that she needed a piece of bread with her breakfast pre-workout, and wanted to eat goat cheese crumbled into a salad she would have at lunch or dinner. We talked about whether she needed either when she had otherwise completely cut bread and dairy out of her diet and was thankful for the results in terms of her weight and, more importantly, how she felt. What she said is that she wanted to create a diet that is sustainable going forward so the D gets capitalized and lasts for her life. She knew her mind, having spent time being introspective, and realized that if she felt too restricted she might crack and give up on eating healthier overall. And she was able to make that decision without throwing in the towel on bread and dairy beyond these two specific cases.

She and I talked about cravings and the *microbiome*. To sum up a subject worthy of many books, we have an ecosystem of good and bad bacteria in our digestive tracts, and these bacteria send chemical signals to our brain to make us crave what they need to survive — for many of the bad ones, this is sugars and starches. When you starve them of this, they start dying and release even stronger craving signals to try to save themselves. Therefore, if you grit it out through a couple of weeks of craving things like bread and sweets, you will likely find that the cravings stop.

As she learned about the cravings that come from these foreign organisms rather than our own body, she said she'd be curious about how to get a cleaner Diet to be sustainable. Can you guess where the conversation went? It went to Do a Day. It can be tough fighting strong cravings for two weeks, when we live in a society with so many quick and cheap ways to answer those cravings. Doing it just for Today is much easier. When you make it to bed, feel your accomplishment. Wake up tomorrow, and Do it the next Day without thinking about how many days have passed or remain.

How do you Do a Day for your Diet? For your health through the food you put into your body? The key is to separate each day and to avoid living in extremes.

That's helpful, general advice, but we need something concrete for you to know where to go from here. We start with the underlying motivation you discovered for yourself, and then think about the goal you set for your future. Ask, "How does my Diet relate to my goal and why I'm going for that goal?" Your answer will be personal and specific to you. Once you have an answer for yourself, you're ready to move on.

Not everyone can wake up and go vegan like I did. I think many more people can than do or that think they can, but the reality is that what I did is too extreme for most people. Instead, what I like to do with my clients, friends and family is to start with something small and manageable that we can adjust in their food choices. Find one thing or one group of foods that you know doesn't constitute good, long-term choices for your health (a common one is soda, including diet soda, which lacks the sugar of regular soda but has tons of nasty chemicals that just aren't helpful for your body). I guide them not to have that thing tomorrow. Wake up, Do a Day of avoiding soda. Don't think about whether you can ever have it again, or whether the soda you've had up to this point has done irreparable damage. Just don't have any Today. And after you Do Today, you wake up the next Day and Do it again. Once you've gone through a month successfully, look to the next smarter choice, and go after it in the same way while maintaining the first choice you made.

The key here is to avoid thinking about not having something for a month or forever, because that can be daunting. You might think about specific situations that will arise that will be hard, or you may let yourself off the hook when the month is up. The reason a month is a good marker is because things generally become a habit after 30 days, so we don't hit that mark and then go back to our old ways. Instead, we take that win and build on it, continuing on that line we began and adding another with an additional good choice.

It's also important not to just think about taking things out of your life. For this to work, it shouldn't just be subtractive. You can look to things to add to your Diet. Specifically, are you eating enough vegetables? That's not the vegan in me sneakily trying to convert you. That's the health coach in me knowing that most people don't eat enough vegetables, especially leafy greens. And some people are kale-obsessed right now, but there are many other great veggies out there that are worth eating. Try adding a leafy green to each meal. There is a long list of options with no right or wrong answers: kale (of course), Swiss chard, collards, lettuce, spinach, arugula, beet greens, dandelion greens or another leafy green. You can't go wrong. Just don't smother it with salad dressing or butter. Steamed or lightly sautéed in a tiny bit of olive or coconut oil and some seasoning such as Himalayan salt, cayenne, turmeric or ginger is great.

Whether it's taking something out or adding something, you go about it the same way. You Do a Day. When you wake up, you focus on the choices you're making for your health just on this Day, and you Do it. When you take out the weight of your entire future, it's much easier to go into today with the resolve and ability to deliver on your goal. When you remove the guilt of the past or longings for a taste you got yesterday, it's easier to make smart choices today.

On the topic of Diet, I want to address something specifically. While I started with soda, another drink is something to strongly consider removing from your life for a variety of reasons — alcohol. I talk about it with a lot of people, and the conversations are usually the same. It's a *huge* source of calories, but perhaps more importantly, it's a source of toxins that your system has to get rid of as a top biological priority. Alcohol is literally poison to your body, which means processing it out of your body prevails over so many other biological functions as your body is a master of survival. That means the energy and time your organs are spending dealing with the alcohol and sugar you put into your system from wine, liquor or beer aren't being spent on making you healthy. That translates to less healing and recovery, removal of cancer-causing free radicals, synthesizing proteins, fighting bacteria and viruses, digesting food and more. It's unproductive work for your body, and I'm certain it doesn't speak to anyone's motivation or goals. The feeling of being hung over is because you've been poisoned, only you did it to yourself.

For me, I was never a big drinker. I drank when I went out on the weekends after graduating from college and had a few hangovers in the mix. But after getting my master's, I backed away from it. As I entered my thirties as a husband and father, I found that I'd maybe have a couple of drinks a year, and they served no real purpose. I didn't have more fun because of them, I didn't care for the taste and I almost always noticed the impact on my health of even one drink. Not to get too graphic, but if you do drink, I want you to pay attention to the smell that you produce in the bathroom the morning after you've had a few drinks. That's a sign that your body is getting poison out of it. In fact, it was this smell that was the wakeup call that drove me to say, "Enough. I don't drink alcohol anymore." After all, what was the point of this small amount of alcohol anyway? If I was barely drinking anymore, and it only had downsides to it, why even bother ever drinking? That was mid-2013 — three years before writing this — and I've not had a drop of alcohol since then. I've not paid a price ever for not having a drop of alcohol in terms of looking weird at social events or feeling like I'm missing out on something. I've only benefited by not weighing my body with that burden anymore, regardless of how big or small the burden was.[24]

The fact is, we don't *need* alcohol, and we do pay a price for having it in our lives. That price is counter to what this book is trying to help with — health, fitness, happiness and balance in life for the rest of your life. This is why I talk about alcohol with people I coach, and why I raise it here. You need to decide what's best for you, but I at least urge you to think about what it is doing to you in any quantity, and whether you need it at all.

---

[24] I can say that I'm not an alcoholic, nor do I have those tendencies. I've never craved alcohol or been unable to say no to it. Therefore, I recognize that it may have been easier for me to stop drinking than for others, and I don't share my story standing in judgment of anyone who drinks. If you do have a problem, I strongly urge you to get help — for yourself and for those who care about you. I promise, no matter how alone you feel, there are people who care about you and want you to be better.

THE END OF THE DAY

Day 13. Do a Day to Eat Well gives you some specific ways to bring better eating habits into your life.

- Diet is about what you eat, every day, for your life, so make smart choices for the long haul rather than short-term, unsustainable or unhealthy decisions

- Making smarter choices boils down to making that choice on a given day, without worrying about whether you chose well yesterday, or whether you will choose well tomorrow

- Good Diet isn't just about taking out unhealthy things, but also adding in healthy foods to ensure you are giving your body what it needs to be its best each day

DAY 14.
DO A DAY FOR LIFE

So here we are at the biggest of all three example areas where Do a Day can help. This chapter will be different from the last two because it isn't about giving you very detailed, specific things you can do for specific situations. It's more to call out the truth of where you are in the process, having gotten this far in the book. The truth is, you are *ready*.

You've read many of my stories of my own struggles and goals, and how Do a Day helped in each one by letting me approach each specific Day, each individual task and each successive goal in turn. I was able to focus on what was right in front of me, all the while appreciating the bigger picture without getting overwhelmed by it. Diet, exercise, parenting, friendship, marriage, work, school — it doesn't matter, the setting or the goal. In each instance, I chose to Do a Day, and through that choice, I was empowered to succeed for the long term.

You, too, can apply Do a Day to the challenges you face in your own life. Beyond the examples I've already shared, I want to list several challenges and a simple idea or two on how to Do a Day to achieve what you truly want to achieve.

Challenge	How to Do a Day
A breakup or divorce	It's OK to hurt, to miss them or to be angry. The good news is that you don't have to feel that way forever, so feel those things today. Explore them today. Allow them today. Tomorrow, find one simple thing to be happy about. Explore that. Allow that. With each day you allow more happiness, you do so at the expense of the pain. With each day,

you grow stronger, happier, more independent. And through the sum of better days, you come out of the situation able to live *your* life and enjoy it as you're meant to.

Chronic illness

To wake each morning in pain and to live with the cloud of "what will get worse tomorrow" is crushing, scary, depressing and fuels anxiety. It is not easy. And when something hurts or gets worse, it is natural to worry about how long it will be that way, or if it will get *even* worse. Instead, focus your mind on the pain or deterioration being today. It doesn't have to hurt tomorrow. Freeing yourself of the weight of tomorrow can allow you to deal with today. To take the pain and try to get through your day. It can allow you the clarity of mind to remember treatments or options you may have to help you endure or improve. You stop being paralyzed by the downward spiral of chronic illness and become more able to cope and even improve. When you do that, you turn a vicious circle into a virtuous cycle, where your improvement gives you hope and a sense of control, which makes you feel emotionally better, which equips you to handle the hardship better. Success builds on itself and you endure and even rise up.

Packing your house and moving

No one likes moving — it's a daunting task that seems to get bigger as you dig deeper into it. I've done it over 10 times myself, so I know all too well. When you look at the task of digging through everything in your house, picking what gets tossed and what gets moved, then packing it safely enough not to get destroyed in transit, the enormity of the task can be crushing. Instead, break the task into pieces — whether room by room ("we'll do the dining room today"), person by person ("pack the kids today") or some other subdivision of your life, it becomes more bearable. Then you have to control the desire to look up, left or right and see the next Day of work. Focus on what you have bitten off for now. Keep your focus on that one thing until you finish before thinking of what else lies ahead. Next thing you know, the house is packed, and you're on your way.

A hard class at school

You look at the syllabus as you realize how tough the teacher or professor is. You add up the pages you'll have to read each night, the pages you'll have to write each week, and the hours of exam studying you'll have to do, and it starts to feel a lot like the marathon training I talked about before, only you don't get a medal or a banana at the end. The solution is much the same — you don't do all the reading at once or write every paper in one sitting. You go through the syllabus one assignment at a time. When you think about it, this one is easy to apply Do a Day to since classes happen on separate days, so you already have the plan in front of you. Don't worry about the total number of pages over the semester. Read what you have to read today. Take in the learning from today with your mind free of the anxiety of all that remains. Not only will you get through it, but you'll learn more and may even enjoy it because you're actively involved and present in the learning process.

The death of a loved one

Losing a loved one is hard no matter how good a life they had or how long it was. While you may have seen it coming or thought you were prepared, it still hits you and it still hurts. You still have a loss, and you still miss them terribly. That's why we call them loved ones. Much like a divorce, you should allow yourself to grieve. And hold that grief in the present day without thinking about how life can go on like this — hurting and without that person. Remember them, and be warmed by the memories. And find something to enjoy. The cliché saying, "They would have wanted it that way," became a cliché because it's used a lot. And it's used a lot because it's true. No one who deserves the term "loved one" would want you to suffer from grief forever. Take the memories and the knowledge that they would want you to love your life as positive points to take with you into each new day in which you find a new reason to be happy.

Sleepless night(s)

It never fails that nights when you find yourself unable to sleep are the nights when you need to sleep the most. They tend to be nights before a big test or event, or come in succession so you get more and more worn down and need sleep more desperately as each night passes. It's understandable in these moments to be worried — about how you can possibly be on your A game in that demanding situation ahead, or how your health is at stake as you spiral downward through exhaustion and the sickness you know you'll get if you don't sleep.

While that's a natural place for your mind to go, it ends up working against your goal of getting sleep. You can't expect sleep to come when you're obsessing about not having it and how bad that is. And whether sleep comes or not, you're making yourself even more exhausted by flooding your body with stress hormones, tensing your muscles and more. Instead, take a breath and try meditating. Instead of focusing on the bad that will ensue, or the piling on of each additional day you won't sleep, focus on right now. Because right now, you can do better. You can at least relax and enjoy the still time in bed, and allow your body to be calm even if it isn't being fully rested. Meditation in the context of restful calm may lead to the sleep that eludes you. And that sleep is likely to be more restful and restorative because of the peaceful way you entered it. Doing this may not be easy, but neither is stressing and worrying, so put that effort into a calming focus on resting your body now rather than worrying about what will happen to your body later.

This set of examples isn't exhaustive, and it's not meant to be. It's meant to share a few other situations you may face in your life, and give some thoughts on how to Do a Day in those situations.

So how do you put it all together? How do you take all the examples I've shared, the concept I've taught through those examples, and apply it to your specific set of Days you want to Do? I'll tell you, sort of.

I want to leave you with questions rather than answers. Questions cause you to think and look within. Answers allow you to go blindly forward under the guidance of someone else. So take each of these questions in turn, think about them — *really think about them* — and answer them for yourself.

We're not having a conversation, so this isn't about giving me the right answer or what you think I want to hear. This is about answering these questions for *yourself*. And if you're not truthful and real with your answers, you will know inside and you will only be cheating yourself. If you are true with your answers and do the deep searching to really answer them, you will walk away empowered and with a very clear sense of what you are going to Do with each Day.

- What do you like about who you are?
- Who matters most to you in your life?
- Do you love yourself? Do you *like* yourself? If not, why? What is it that's keeping you from feeling that way? And what are you going to do to work on those things?
- What kind of person do you want to be a year from now? Five years from now? Twenty?
    - o Why do you want this to be who you are? That is, what is *driving* this desire?
    - o How can you get there? What goals can you set going forward to make this happen?
- What do you want to be better in your life today? In 10, 20 or more years?
    - o Why do you want this thing or these things to be better?
    - o What is the motivation behind this desire?
    - o What goal can you set around this? That is, how can *you* make it better?

These are deep questions with deep answers. Some will help you discover your real motivation, some will help define your goals and some will help you to know yourself better. These are not the only questions to ask yourself, but they will help you with your introspective journey — the journey you have to go through to create a life of success.

When you get to a place of understanding yourself, what you want and why you want it, you can define what you will do to get it. That definition is the set of actions you are going to Do. So, see your goal, break it into a Day, and you now have your call to action for Tomorrow.

All that's left is to go and get it. You know what it takes, you understand why it works and you know yourself. You know the path to success that lies ahead and you're excited to be on that path. Now, you know what you need to do:

Do a Day.

IV. YOUR TOMORROW

So, let me leave by asking you a question — what will you Do with your next Day? What will you make Tomorrow about? What do you want to achieve, overcome or *become*? I hope you can use this book to go after what you truly want, driven by your true motivation, and create a complete, satisfying, healthy life.

I don't want to just have you go off and do that in a vacuum. I want to help and hear from you on that journey. I've put together a little exercise to help you get started at www.doadaybook.com/theexercise.

You can work with me to help coach you through the process. To learn more about coaching options, just visit www.doadaybook.com/coaching.

I want to ask something else of you: I want to hear from you about how you **Do a Day**, and what you have achieved through it. Your story can help inspire others as you become part of the growing Do a Day community. While my personal examples can help, the more varied the stories of success, the more power Do a Day can have by applying to an even broader audience and set of goals and challenges. Sharing your story can be done confidentially and anonymously if you want, and it comes with absolutely no judgment or comparison to others. It's just about what matters to you, and how Do a Day helped. Please visit www.doadaybook.com/share to share your story.

V. MY TOMORROW

What's next for me? What is the Tomorrow that I will Do?

I have three things I want to achieve from here, and they're big. They are also things with clear actions and steps I can take every day, and I can focus on what I need to achieve each day while I win my way to success.

1. Do a Day Full-Time

I want to use this book to help as many people as I can. I hope that many people choose to read this book and take the message forward in their own lives. I want to do more coaching work so I can really dig in with individuals on how to go after what they hope to achieve. I'd love to have the opportunity to speak to large groups of people to help spread the message of Do a Day, and inspire even more people. Ultimately, in an ideal world, I would do this full time. I love my day job and work for an incredible company I don't want to leave and could (very) happily stay at until I retire. But if there is a way to help people full-time and get to inspire real improvements in people's lives, that would be my ideal career.

2. Share Other People's Days

As I succeed in my first goal above, I want to use that to be a bullhorn for others. I want to move beyond my own story, and write a follow-up book to *Do a Day* that compiles the most inspiring stories from you and get those stories out to inspire an even broader population of people who want better for themselves but need help getting there. If you share your story with me, I can give you a voice to help inspire others through the platform of Do a Day. So please do visit www.doadaybook.com/share and tell me your story.

3. Finish an Ironman Triathlon

I have wanted to tackle the Ironman since I started riding a road bike in 2013. There's something so profound and challenging about it, and it's such a huge piece of proof to myself that I've truly conquered my past as "the fat kid." I have told people I want to do that, but always said I needed to complete a marathon first.

Well, I did that Day, so it's time for Tomorrow.

I can look at the gravity of it all, and cower into doing nothing. Instead, I am going to map the Days that I need to Do to accomplish this. As I've said time and time again across this entire book, this is the path to success. I haven't done a single thing by staring at the end and the mountain of things to do to reach that end. No. I plotted a course, and then took one step at a time without worrying about the distance and obstacles that were between me and the end.

I will build a training plan. That plan will tell me exactly what I need to Do each Day so I can build my way to that finish line to hear the words, "Bryan Falchuk, YOU ARE AN IRONMAN."

It's no different from writing this book. I'm not an author, I struggled in English class growing up and I don't have contacts in publishing. I don't know Oprah. And yet here we are at the end of the book, and the fact that you're reading this means I've figured out the pieces and gotten the help I need to get it out there.

So stay tuned — there are more Days for me to Do, and I plan to share them with you in a real way. My dreams have been "impossible" when I looked at them in their entirety before I started to attack them. But I've achieved each one so far, as I will with the next one. And the ones after that. Because I know how to Do them. And now, you do, too.

And with that, I'll leave you again with the one question that matters most: What will you Do with your next Day?

ACKNOWLEDGEMENTS

I'm thankful for so many people and opportunities in my life – my family, friends, teachers and so many others. When it comes to this book, I want to start with five specific people who have had a pivotal impact on my journey at very crucial times. Without them, their support, motivation, challenge, guidance and inspiration, not only would this book not exist but the idea behind it would never have been formed. I don't mention them in order of importance as the truth is I needed all five of them plus an army of others to get where I am.

First is Henri Andre, the P.E. teacher and coach from my high school. As I mentioned in *From "The Fat Kid" to "A Fit Man"*, Mr. Andre gave me the tools I needed to start my journey, and did so in a way that made me actually want to learn to use them. No one else had been able to spark the interest to be healthy before I met him, and he remains someone I hold in the highest esteem. His positive attitude, caring approach, (massive) wealth of knowledge and genuine dedication to inspiring teens to want to be healthier for themselves makes him truly invaluable in this world. For being the catalyst and first guide for my change to living a better life, *Merci*, Henri!

Second is Matt Mirisola. Matt is an executive coach I was lucky to be connected with as part of my professional development at a prior job. Matt and I connected so quickly and so well that he was able to guide me to understand myself at a time I really needed it most. He helped me get deep down under the surface of why I am who and how I am, what power that can create for me, and what I need to be careful of as a result. In addition to helping me understand myself and my motivation in a way I didn't think anyone could, Matt also ignited in me the spark to want to help others with their own self-understanding, -growth and -betterment.

Third is Dai Manuel. As I began my permanent health journey in 2011, I found this energetic, inspiring, driven Canadian who used to be obese just like me. Only he had an army of tens of thousands of people following him on social media, appeared regularly on TV and radio, and was inspiring countless people to better their lives. I tweeted something while mentioning his name, and he wrote back within minutes. I was like a giddy little kid who just got a new toy. And that wasn't the last time I heard from him. Dai has always been right there, quick to come back to me, offer me guidance, help me grow my own business and support me in whatever endeavor I've been on since connecting with him. It's funny that we have yet to meet in person as I write this, yet I count him as one of the people I'm closest to because of how quickly and meaningfully we connected. This is partially because of our similar backstories and dreams for how to live our lives, but primarily because of the type of human being Dai is. The main reason Dai deserves acknowledgement here is because he is literally the catalyst for the book. Despite being in the middle of launching his own book and packing his family up to live on the road for a year, Dai gave me over an hour of his time to just talk and offer help however he could for me and my life. That mentoring call is where the idea for the book was created. He helped me draw out what my true dream is, and then helped me work backward for how to get there. I was really moved by the call, and found myself overcome with clarity, purpose and drive. I woke up early the next morning and went for a run along the San Francisco waterfront (the piers along the Embarcadero, for those who know the area), and I kept working through what we had talked about. It became so clear to me that I had to write a book, and I knew *exactly* what it would be about. I even planned the outline in my head during the run. I got back to my hotel, hit the shower, packed, went to the airport and immediately started writing right there in the terminal, and kept writing through my long flight home. By the afternoon, I had the entire book structure on paper, and the first three chapters drafted. Dai is the spark that started the fire of this book, and I can't thank him enough. And if you appreciated reading this and what Do a Day can do for your life, you, too, should be unable to thank him enough!

Fourth is my amazing, gorgeous wife, Sharon (I know reading me describe her that way isn't going to sit well with her, but the words are just facts). She is one of the strongest people in the world and has been through so much, yet endured. Where others might quit and despite others quitting on her or blowing her off, she persevered and found the path to wellness herself. And she brought me and our son along for the ride. We all live better thanks to her efforts and her caring. I also know that, without her hard work, I would be just like most other middle-aged American men – going through life automatically with ever-deteriorating levels of health and fitness. We've been on quite a journey together and hit plenty of bumps in the road, but we're smarter for it, healthier for it, better parents for it, and in a lot of ways closer for it. Sharon, I loved you the moment I saw you, and love you every bit as much today. Thank you.

Of the people who played major roles here, the last one I'll mention is the most important – my son. He is my reason. He is my motivation. He is honestly the most amazing human being I've ever met. He's kind, thoughtful, incredibly intelligent, fun, imaginative and driven. His smile makes everyone else smile – and he smiles a lot. The most important thing I've ever done and ever will do is to be his father, and I don't take that responsibility lightly. And rather than seeing it as a responsibility – something you *have* to do – I see it as an opportunity I've been blessed with. Buddy, I know I tell you a lot, but I love you more than anything and owe you so much. You literally saved me and gave me this better, healthier, happier life. I hope you look at me with love, pride and admiration because that's how I look at you. You inspire me and deserve everything I can give you.

Beyond these individual people, this book wouldn't be possible without some specific contributors to the process. Christine Schuldt (www.pinstripepartnersllc.com), Becki Ledford (www.fightingforwellness.com), Christie Manuel (Dai's wife, and an equally amazing person), and Matt Stein were such helpful friend-editors, giving great, critical feedback and catching many of the mistakes I couldn't see myself! You are reading this book because of the contributions and efforts of these people, and they deserve thanks and recognition.

I also want to thank Gary Smailes at BubbleCow, my professional editor on this book. Gary saw my vision for the book, and appreciated the way I wanted to tell it. He guided me to create structure and flow to the book without losing the conversational, comfortable tone and style I wanted to use – no small feat! Gary gave such great feedback and support, and clearly went over and above what his official obligations were as a paid editor of this book.

OK, one last acknowledgement. You! For everyone who bought this book, engaged in meaningful conversation with me about your own self-growth and aspiration for a better life, I am so grateful that you trusted me to be on that journey with you. I hope this book has lived up to your expectations and given you what you need to **Do a Day**.

ABOUT THE AUTHOR

Bryan Falchuk is a Certified Personal Trainer and Behavior Change Specialist based in the Boston area, where he founded newbodi.es to help people change their lives for the better. He is a husband, father, brother, uncle, son, and many other things. Bryan spent the first half of his life obese, and much of the second half trying not to be obese again until he

© Lindsey Forg

discovered the approach to change all that – *Do a Day*. Using Do A Day, Bryan was able to break from this pattern to live a life of consistent, unending health and wellness, and works to share what he's learned with others seeking a happier, more complete existence through newbodi.es. As Bryan says, people don't change, lives do. His goal is to help people change their lives.

Bryan changed his life while staying true to himself. So can you. Tomorrow is a new Day for all of us. You can wake up and Do it.

Follow Do a Day!

Web: www.doadaybook.com

Twitter: @doadaybook & @newbodi

Instagram: @doadaybook & @newbodi

Facebook: www.facebook.com/doadaybook
                   www.facebook.com/newbodies

45759650R00082

Made in the USA
Middletown, DE
12 July 2017